TOO CLOSE TO CALL

An Insider's View of the GOP's Push for Political
Power in Congress

SARATOGA

DAN BAZILE

ZTRUTH
A ZLS Publishing Imprint
Albany, NY

Published by ZLS Publishing, a division of The Z Group, 255 Orange Street, Suite 207, Albany, NY 12210.
(518) 772-4718.

For more information about ZLS Publishing, visit our website at: www.zlspublishing.com
To buy books from our authors, visit our store at: www.zlspublishing.com/shop

Distributed in the USA, Canada, and the UK.

Cover Illustration by: Rich Gabriel
Edited by: Natanya Housman

ISBN 978-098459-863-2

Library of Congress Cataloging in -Publication Data application submitted.

*To my beautiful wife and daughter,
and to my friend Rick Kissane*

Table of Contents

Table of Contents
Narrative

Election Night:

This was the moment that changed it all. This was the moment when James N. Tedisco and his entourage learned their fate, or so it seemed. His staff, his wife and everyone who surrounded him on election night had a feeling the race was headed in the other direction. They watched the ballot count on television inside a hotel room. The tension was extremely high. Tedisco talked about what he could have done differently to run a better campaign. But the stage was already set. The odds were clearly against his opponent Scott Murphy. However the political newcomer was having a really good night thanks to President Barack Obama's long coattails.

Creating a Vacancy:

The battle for New York's 20th Congressional District seat began with a chain of events that nearly defied logic. Tedisco wasn't even thinking about running until Hillary Clinton gave up her Senate seat in New York to become Secretary of State for the Obama Administration. The daughter of Camelot Caroline Kennedy was set to replace her. However, New York Governor David Paterson, whose responsibility was to appoint Clinton's successor in the Senate, botched the whole process which fueled a lot of controversy. Patterson snubbed Kennedy and picked little known Congresswoman Kirsten Gillibrand from New

York's 20th District to replace Clinton instead. That's when Tedisco decided to make a run for the seat – confident he would win it. Scott Murphy popped out of nowhere to challenge Tedisco. Murphy's biggest ammunition was no other than President Barack Obama.

The Urge to Run:

Once Tedisco decided to become a candidate, his colleagues started calling him congressman because there was no question he would come out on top. It didn't matter that Republican candidates were having trouble every where in the county. It didn't matter that President Obama was enjoying some of the highest approval ratings ever seen. It didn't matter that even some Republicans didn't like the direction the GOP was headed. Tedisco was going for it. Besides, he had been after that district for a long time. This was his chance. This was his moment. He had sacrificed enough for the GOP. The 20th Congressional District was his reward.

Selecting a Candidate:

The Republicans were divided. Since the 20th Congressional District was historically GOP Territory, Republicans felt the seat rightfully belongs to them. Tedisco was one of three possible candidates who wanted the easy win. There's no primary in a special election. The Republican county chairs where the district lines fall, had a choice between three old time politicians. When they picked Tedisco, obviously the other two possible candidates were angry. They campaigned against Tedisco during the entire election. The Democrats, on the other hand, did the opposite. It took them a long time to make their choice. They collected resumes and conducted interviews. In the end, when the county chairs picked Scott Murphy, everyone was a bit surprised since he was so new at the political game.

Building a Message:

Scott Murphy released the first television commercial in the race. It stunned Tedisco and his staff. Murphy appeared to be a serious contender. He was a natural in front of a camera and he seemed genuine. That could be a problem. After both men introduced themselves to the district in a few friendly and beautiful ads, the gloves came off. Tedisco launched the first attack, a move he would end up regretting later on. The rest of the election was focused mainly on President Obama's stimulus program. The president had just signed the bill into law. The critical question was how Tedisco would have voted for the stimulus program as a congressman. Tedisco waffled on the answer and gave his opponent a lethal weapon.

PREFACE

I was naive. I thought I understood politics after covering it for years as a reporter at the State Capitol in New York. My experience on the inside was an awakening of sorts – a light bulb flashed inside my brain. It was as if I was a teenager. Most teenagers think they know everything – that they're invincible. They may also believe that their parents are idiots. But once they grow up, they often find out that parents are actually geniuses and that they, as children, knew nothing at all. That's the way I felt. I only knew a fraction of what was going on in this peculiar world of senators, representatives, governors, and presidents.

I certainly loved covering politics as a television reporter. When I first jumped into it, I uncovered government waste for a television station in Albany, New York. Albany is a political city. It's the capital of New York State where many of its residents are making a living on the government dime, one way or another. Some work for private contractors that are, in turn, working on state projects.

Others work for quasi-public agencies. Many of those organizations are called authorities and don't consider themselves government entities but their massive debts are ultimately in the hands of New York taxpayers. You can imagine why people in Albany would be interested in government and policies and why Albany and politics are comparable to Detroit and the car industry. You can't be a journalist in the Motor City without covering the car manufacturers just like you can't be a news source in Albany without writing about politicians.

It was a fairly easy beat because the Capitol was a constant source of news. Lawmakers and some of the people around them were always getting into trouble. I remember my first big scandal at the Capitol. Former Chief Counsel for the State Assembly Speaker was accused of raping a 22-year-old legislative aide. J. Michael Boxley's arrest was caught on tape and blasted all over the six o'clock news. I was one of many journalists on the scene, gathering information. We were like a bunch of kids in a candy store. The 43-year-old Boxley was the Chief Counsel to a very powerful man in government – Assembly Speaker Sheldon Silver.

Nothing seemed to get accomplished in Albany without his approval. He had the biggest majority behind him, so votes to pass bills he supported went through like a breeze. And there he was, his Chief Counsel, the person who was supposed to know the law best, breaking it, and he was arrested in disgrace. You couldn't make it up, not even in a bestselling novel. Boxley was indicted by a grand jury. He temporarily lost his law license in 2004 after admitting to a lower charge.

Little did I know, the Boxley matter would pale in comparison to what would follow. It was as if Albany was cursed. The stories kept getting worse and worse. There was the Hevesi scandal. Former State Comptroller Alan Hevesi was convicted on a felony corruption charge for defrauding the government. As State Comptroller, Hevesi was considered the money man, the person who looked over the state's finances and made sure they were sound. He paid the bills for the state. He also looked after the state's pension fund with billions of dollars in assets. Hevesi was caught using state workers as his wife's chauffeur and personal assistant. Despite the embarrassment just around election time, Hevesi was reelected. He pleaded guilty in 2006 and resigned. But Hevesi served no jail time and continued to get paid more than $100,000 a year from his state pension. The stories went on and on, just like that.

As a watchdog, I uncovered some corruptions of my own and embarrassed a few politicians along the way. Seven years into it, I felt that I had seen it all. I was comfortable and well-informed with anything political, both state and national. I kept my eye on Washington. There were plenty of stories about wasteful spending inside the beltway. Every year I had fun writing about earmarks in Congress and the various political pet projects for which the money was used. There was money to study the behavior of certain animals that posed no threat to humans. There was money to promote American culture and heritage. There was cash to study ocean wildlife. Well, you get the idea.

I was becoming an authority on the subject of government.

No matter how much I thought I knew about politics, nothing could have prepared me to take a look behind the curtain. It's kind of like *The Wizard of Oz* when Dorothy, the Cowardly Lion, the Tin Man, and the Scarecrow found out what was behind the curtain. They didn't know they were being deceived until they saw an ordinary man posing as the Wizard. But that was just for fun. The fake wizard meant no harm. Politics, on the other hand, can be a nasty game. Some people call it a blood sport. The problem is real people get hurt. The effects can last for a long time because once a law is in place, it's harder to get rid of it.

So I left the television spotlight for a bit. With the curiosity of a reporter, I lifted the curtain and joined the blood sport from the inside. I was like an embedded journalist with a front row seat to New York State's history in the making. It was a lot of fun at first. Instead of reporting news, I was making it happen as a Communications Advisor to a politician. I knew what was coming down the pike before everybody else. I had the inside track and real access to firsthand information. I would read a news article and think of ten different angles the reporter could have taken to make it better based on my new insider knowledge. I was back in the candy store checking out different flavors of so many stories.

The only trouble was, I couldn't tell anyone. I was one of them now – them, the politicians who recruited me. I was in high-level meetings, listening to these lawmakers pontificate and accomplish nothing. Pointless meetings did take place on a regular basis, believe it or not. There were get-togethers about absolutely nothing at all. People talked, and others listened, while burying their heads in their smart phones. What were they doing, playing with their phones? Upon closer examination, I found many of them were just acting important. Some were answering random e-mails, while others were checking news headlines or Google alerts about themselves.

I did miss the days when I was free to talk about those politicians, and thousands would watch, listen, or read my reports on the Internet. Journalism is somewhat intoxicating. Once it gets into your bloodstream, it's hard to get rid of the urge. It gets even more tempting whenever big news stories break. When former New York Governor Eliot Spitzer resigned amid a prostitution scandal, I would sit in my office dreaming of all the things I could tell the television audience. I missed the spotlight then. I felt like a stranger in the strange land of public service. I questioned whether I belonged there. That was to be expected with any new job, I thought. I had a pretty good journalism career. Why did I leave? What was I looking for? I couldn't answer those questions.

Then there was the State Senate coup. Democrats had just gained control of the State Senate by a slim majority. Two Democrats split to join the Republicans. That gave the Senate back to the GOP. It was short-lived. The two dissident Democrats went back to their party about a month later. Democrats were in charge once again. If that sounds confusing, that's because it was. The power grab created a big mess and gridlock at the Capitol. It served as an embarrassment to New York State. Stories like that were more fun to cover as a journalist. What good was it to have inside information and not be able to tell the world about it?

The highlight of my short stint in government came in the form of a federal election. I was thrust in the middle of a congressional campaign with political insiders from Washington. That race turned out to be one of the most fascinating congressional elections in history. The two candidates faced off in the dog fight for the 20th Congressional District in New York. The race was played out in national news. I was there every step of the way, serving as a quasi-Communications Advisor to one of the candidates. But I was more like an observer, an embedded reporter listening to every conversation.

Months later, I was back on television news with a passion to share my experience. The year and a half in state government felt more like a decade. So much had happened in that small span of time. The first African American had become president. New York's governor had resigned, making way for the first black and visually impaired governor. Republicans everywhere had a tough time getting elected. The economy was tanking. Americans were losing their homes to foreclosure at an alarming rate. The rich were getting richer. It all became clear. I understood exactly why so many Americans were angry. I knew why they all wanted something to change. If they all had a chance to pull the curtain back, like I did, and take a peek inside, they'd probably be even more outraged. That's why I decided to write this book.

PART I -
PRE-ELECTION

Election Night

It was fairly warm for a March day in the Northeast. The sun was just about to set on a day that made the cold winter seemed like a distant past. But the mood was still cold inside a Holiday Inn hotel suite in Saratoga Springs, NY. That's where James N. Tedisco and his entourage sat in suspense to watch the election returns determine their future. Political elections normally didn't take place in March. Voting in November was a more customary method. This was a special contest for a vacant seat in the House of Representatives. Tedisco, pacing back and forth, stopped at the sound of each update from the Board of Elections with measured optimism.

"Tedisco up by 100 votes in Saratoga," someone would shout. Then minutes later, a different voice would say, "Columbia County is killing us." Tedisco never took election night for granted. He was always anxious, even when he ran for elected office unopposed. The last time his name was on a ballot, he spent most of his time campaigning and worrying about the outcome without an opponent.

He agonized over the idea that he'd still lose if voters decided not to vote for him at all but this time around, he had a viable opponent, and it seemed that he was unable to hold it together. He looked uncomfortable and squeamish. Perhaps the worst feeling was to think that there was nothing else he could do to change the outcome. "If I had just knocked on one more door, that would have been another vote," he said. The polls had closed. The votes were in. At that point, Tedisco could have screamed from the mountaintop any legitimate reason why he was a better candidate for Congress than Scott Murphy. It wouldn't have made any difference.

Room service knocked on the hotel suite door with what smelled like an order of chicken wings. But this was not Sunday Night Football. This was a night that could make or break careers. After weeks of campaigning and more than 26 years in the New York State Assembly without ever losing an election, it all came down to this night for Tedisco. A congressional seat was on the line. One night going head-to-head with a political rookie could end his winning streak. It could also mean the end of the road for his seat in the Assembly.

He often talked about retiring from public service if the Congressional race didn't pan out. His staff, some of whom had been with him for two decades, could also find themselves on the unemployment line if Tedisco lost this race. The numbers flashing across the screen from a television on top of an armoire in the corner of the room were   scary and enough to kill anyone's appetite. The race was neck and neck.

On the other side of the hotel room, Tedisco's top staff was following the numbers on laptops. "I have numbers for Greene County," a staffer would say. "I got the numbers for Warren," another would exclaim. County Boards of Elections provided a play-by-play of the numbers online. The refresh buttons on those laptops were nearly worn out by the end of the night. It was a tug-of-war between happy cheers and churning stomachs after every stroke of the keys. It was as if you were standing in the middle of the floor of the New York Stock Exchange. People were yelling uncontrollably at each other while staring at computer screens, nervously waiting for the numbers to change.

Downstairs in a banquet room, a crowd of Tedisco supporters waited patiently as they helped themselves to drinks and finger foods. "This race seemed close, way too close," one woman said with a drink in one hand and a blank stare on her face. Room chatter drowned out the music blasting from a pair of giant speakers. In one corner, some Tedisco supporters huddled together. You could feel the heat of the tension emanating from their body language. Confidence had slowly started to fade. But the group remained largely optimistic that their nominee would eventually squeak this one out. On the local television screens, set up for the television reporters, Tedisco was up. Then Murphy quickly took the lead. Then it was Tedisco's turn on top once again. The lead went back and forth like a ping-pong ball for most of the night. No one could predict where the race was headed.

Some considered the possibility of a real tie where each candidate would end up with exactly the same amount of votes. The polls did suggest such an outcome, but reality was starting to sink in for many on Tedisco's team. Murphy was having a good night for a political newcomer. Heck, he might even win this. Tedisco was starting to lose ground in areas where the campaign team thought he'd be competitive against Murphy. It just seemed like he didn't have the numbers to pull through. Some people were visibly worried while trying to conjure up fake smiles. With only forty percent of the precincts reporting, it seemed that there was plenty of time left.

Back upstairs in the hotel room where Tedisco and his campaign staff hunkered down, the chicken wings were now cold. No one touched them. The crew was busy crunching numbers from different counties. It became clear that Saratoga was the county to watch. That was where Tedisco concentrated his campaign. Saratoga County residents already knew him well. They were used to seeing his name on the ballot because part of his New York State Assembly district was in Saratoga County. A big margin of victory there would have, in all likelihood, delivered a win for Tedisco. The cheers grew louder each time the numbers went in Tedisco's favor. "We're smoking 'em," an aide said, referring to Murphy but the room would remain quiet when Tedisco was tanking. The clicks from the laptops' refresh buttons intensified as more precincts checked in. "How are the numbers in Saratoga?" Tedisco asked, his pacing more labored.

On the television screen, the local news was live at Murphy's headquarters at Gideon Putnam in Saratoga Springs. New York State Governor David Paterson and then newly appointed Senator Kirsten Gillibrand were both closely watching the drama unfold with Murphy. Some Tedisco supporters pointed to what was perceived as a role reversal for the two parties. Political party stereotypes dictate that Republicans fight for the rich and Democrats fight against the rich for the common man. It seemed that this race was taking place in an alternate universe. The two candidates had it backwards: Murphy, the Democrat, was a millionaire venture capitalist and chose Gideon Putnam – an upscale restaurant and spa to greet his supporters. Tedisco, the Republican, was seen as the common man, the one who didn't have millions of dollars in the bank and most likely understood the middle class. He picked Holiday Inn for his election night rally.

Political observers also pointed out the lack of business support for Murphy, the successful businessman. All the labor unions backed his candidacy, while pro-business groups threw their support behind Tedisco, the apparent middle-class candidate. Murphy's supporters appeared lively on election night. They were eating and dancing. Their nominee, who at first glance had no chance with a veteran politician, materialized into a top-notch competitor on the verge of a major upset. They had accomplished what was nearly impossible. They had come this far with a candidate who was down 21 points in the polls and had to build his name recognition from scratch.[1] They were up against a well-known and formidable opponent in a district where Democrats had been the minority for years. But Murphy's campaign had a lot of energy spilled over from the nomination and the election of Democratic President Barack Obama.

They probably would have accepted defeat since the majority of people expected Tedisco to win anyway.[2] The goal for Democrats, it seemed, was to make a good effort in hopes of setting things up for the next election. Whatever the outcome, Tedisco's team assumed the Murphy campaign already felt like winners. An actual win would be icing on the cake.

One quick look at Tedisco's face in the room, and you could see an overtired man with billions of thoughts racing through his mind at light speed. He'd been functioning on just a few naps that he had taken in his car between campaign stops. Who could really sleep anyway when so much was at stake? The Congressional race had become bigger than the two candidates. The national media was all over the District, framing the race as a comeback for the Republican Party or a possible referendum on President Obama's policies.[3]

Speculations were rampant that a win for Murphy would spell more disaster for Republicans. The GOP took a beating in the 2006 midterm elections. That was the end of their majority in Congress since the party took over in 1994. Before that, Republicans had not held the majority in the house for four decades. Then in November 2008, there was more disappointment for the GOP brought on by eight years of Republican President George W. Bush.

The GOP had lost all political power in Washington. The local election had quickly turned into a movement for Republicans. Congressional leaders, like John Boehner, were on the phone with Tedisco every chance they could get during the campaign, raising money wherever they could find it. The entire country, it seemed, was watching with bated breath to get a real sense of voters' attitudes towards President Obama and Republicans.

President Obama's political skills have been put to the test before. His then young administration had to maneuver its way through the powers in Washington to confirm many of his cabinet members. Some of them did things, such as not paying their taxes, creating a scandal for the young admin-istration.[4] Obama had to apologize over and over again after taking responsibility for the scandal. His popularity increased according to the polls. To many

Americans, he became the President who recognized his mistakes, unlike the previous one.

Polls are just samples, and voters tend to think independently when they're in the voting booth, casting their ballot. The race for New York's 20th Congressional District would become the first real political test for the new president. It was a choice between those who loved Obama's policies and those who thought his policies would harm the country. The President had become a major focus in the race. Murphy embraced the President's every move. Tedisco disliked most of what the new White House had to offer Americans.

Meanwhile, Murphy took a small lead over Tedisco. It sucked the air out of the Saratoga Springs hotel suite. One campaign aide briefly stepped out, perhaps to try to absorb the first major blow of the night. Tedisco was down by about 300 votes – a real scary moment for the campaign. "I don't know if we can pull this off, guys," said the campaign's Communications Director in another room. "The trend doesn't look good. We should be up by a lot more in Saratoga County by now if we expect to win," he said with anxiety. Saratoga County did look somewhat promising for Tedisco earlier in the night. Many of the precincts that had yet to report their results were said to be Republican strongholds. It was the one glimmer of hope that would somehow turn things around for Tedisco. Pessimism was starting to rear its ugly head. Moments later, a huge sigh of relief came when the

Board of Elections corrected a mistake in the numbers, giving Tedisco more than 200 extra votes. With 60% of the precincts reporting, the race was too close to call. Murphy and Tedisco were separated by about 100 votes. No one's lead was getting any bigger, even as more votes were thrown into the count. Saratoga County didn't come through for Tedisco. His margin there wasn't enough to push him over the edge. Murphy was also ahead by bigger margins in the counties he won over Tedisco. The chatter in the hotel room subsided. All signs of a victory party for Tedisco over Murphy faded.

When the counting was finally over, only 60 votes separated the two men. Voters simply couldn't make up their minds. One man at a polling place said that he actually flipped a coin before going into the voting booth. He blamed negative campaigning and the economy for his indecision. He didn't have a clue of who between Tedisco and Murphy would be best suited to fix America's financial problem. Both sides had anticipated a low turnout, given that elections didn't ordinarily take place in March. "Maybe 25% will show up," one local official said the day before. But this special Congressional race was different. People were paying close attention, partly because of a constant barrage of television advertisements. More than 35% of registered voters went to the polls, breaking special election records for the past decade in the United States.[5] On average, voter turnout for special elections in the 20th

Congressional District has been around 91,000.[6] More than 160,000 people went to the polls for Murphy and Tedisco. Nonetheless, the race was far from over. The deciding factor would be up to the nearly 7,000 absentee ballots that were left to be counted a week after the election. That's not the way it was supposed to happen – at least not for Tedisco. For those who knew him, election night was meant to be the climax of his political career. To them, Tedisco was already the winner. The election was a mere formality. The idea of a newcomer, like Murphy, taking away what seemed rightfully his was troubling to the entire Republican Party. The thought that a veteran Republican couldn't embarrass a political unknown in a Conservative Republican district made GOP leaders reflect on their inability to connect with voters.

The time had come to address the supporters. "We're not going to concede," Tedisco muttered with a hoarse voice and very little energy. The concession speech was set aside. With a slightly altered victory speech and his wife Mary Song by his side, Tedisco slowly strolled into an elevator, his entourage in tow. In the hotel lobby, a group of young Republicans erupted in cheers and claps as Tedisco walked by. He was on his way to give one of the most important speeches of his life. No one had imagined this moment. There were mixed emotions. Supporters in the banquet room were thrilled when they spotted Tedisco but they couldn't hide their sorrow. Tedisco walked through the crowd, shaking hands along the way. Lights, flashes, and cameras captured it all – a moment he'll never forget.

Even though he was tired and feeling nearly defeated, he put on a pretty good performance. You could always count on him to do that. He would find that last bit of reserved energy in front of a crowd. That night was no different. The room went silent. Supporters and more than a half a dozen television cameras were looking back at Tedisco on the podium. You could hear a pin drop in the few seconds he took to gather his thoughts. Then he opened up with the usual joke. "You could call me Landslide Tedisco," he said.

Creating a Vacancy

T he battle for New York's 20th Congressional District between Tedisco and Murphy began a few months prior to the election, with a chain of events that nearly defied logic. Tedisco was busy making plans for his leadership role in the New York State Assembly. He was the in-your-face loyal opposition and happy to be in that position. Nothing pleased him more than to take a shot at Democrats, especially when he felt the GOP had a better, more populous message. The state budget was shaping up to be one of his biggest fights ever in 2009. New York was deep in the red with mounting debts and a growing deficit.

The Democrats had taken full control of the State, vowing to fix the problem for New Yorkers. All statewide offices were in the hands of Democrats, with some towns and villages following the same trend. Tedisco was sharpening his claws to take on the dysfunctional state legislature. With Democrats fully in charge, he could be much more critical of the establishment. When Republicans controlled the New York State Senate, Tedisco had to be careful not to hurt his fellow GOP members when he launched his attacks. Now, Tedisco could be as nasty as possible.

National Republicans, on the other hand, were just trying to figure out a way to rebuild their party and develop a message that could resonate with the middle class. They were picking up the pieces after some devastating election losses across the country. Tedisco was more than willing to help improve the party's image. New York's 20th Congressional District didn't even cross his mind. At least, that's what he'd been saying.

No one knew who Scott Murphy was, except perhaps his family, business associates, and circle of friends. The venture capitalist was not completely new to politics. He was a volunteer for the Clinton '92 campaign during his last year at Harvard University. He had worked for two Missouri Governors, Mel Carnahan and Roger Wilson, but he had never held public office. The Glens Falls Civic Center, a venue for sports and entertainment, in the District in which Murphy lived, was where he made his biggest public decision as a board member. It seemed that he popped out of nowhere and thrust himself into New York politics. It was a long shot for both candidates. According to published reports, Murphy's family was stunned when they found out he was running for Congress. They thought he would go for a much smaller office, like mayor or city council for his first crack at public office. But Murphy, it seemed, had bigger aspirations. Tedisco, on the other hand, was comfortable as a state lawmaker. He had indicated that he would most likely retire from the State Legislature. The odds of Tedisco and Murphy facing off in a congressional race had to have been worse than the odds of a person getting struck by lighting.

First, former First Lady Hillary Rodham Clinton unsuccessfully ran for president in 2008. When she announced her candidacy two years before the election, the majority of Americans thought she'd be the first woman Commander In Chief. Many pundits said she was measuring the drapes for the Oval Office before the first caucus. New York Governor David Paterson, the Lieutenant Governor at the time, would have been the likely candidate to replace Mrs. Clinton in the U.S. Senate. Many political observers believe that former Governor Eliot Spitzer would have appointed him. Paterson was pulling for Clinton to become president. He didn't endorse President Barack Obama. But in early March 2008, Spitzer crashed and burned and had to resign after he was caught in a prostitution ring (see Chapter 5).

The nation was shocked. Paterson was sworn in as New York's first black governor. Then Americans were shocked once again when Clinton lost the Democratic nomination to Obama in early June 2008. She and President Obama clashed in a made-for-TV combat for the nomination to face off with Republican John McCain. Obama, who appeared to be out of his league at first, made history by beating the odds to become the first African American President of the United States. Clinton resigned her U.S. Senate seat in New York to take the Secretary of State position in her former rival's administration.

Her vacant seat generated a lot of national interests when President John F. Kennedy's daughter, Caroline Kennedy, jumped into the crowded field of candidates to fill the post. Little-known Congresswoman Kirsten Gillibrand barely registered on the radar screen as a possible pick. As far as New Yorkers were concerned, Kennedy was a shoo-in. The door seemed wide open for the former first daughter even though she had never before held political office. Her name was extremely powerful and influential.

Republicans would be afraid to challenge her re-election bid. She had helped Obama during his campaign for president. She also would have been the second member of her family to represent New York in the Senate. Her uncle, Robert Kennedy, held the same seat in the 1960s. So, she was essentially the perfect candidate. Yet, she was still a novice who didn't do well in her first round of media interviews. Critics, mostly other selected officials who wished they were being considered for the job, pointed to her lack of experience as a problem. "Kennedy has name recognition, but so does J.Lo. I wouldn't make J.Lo the Senator unless she proved she had great qualifications, but we haven't seen them yet," one critic said. J.Lo refers to Jennifer Lopez, a popular Hispanic singer and actress.[7]

New York Governor David Paterson was the sole per son with the power to appoint Clinton's successor. Possessing the ability to appoint a U.S. senator is complicated.[8] The decision is not always based on what people want, but rather on what would work best for the person making the appointment. Ex-Illinois Governor Rod Blagojevich took some heat after being accused of trying to sell the Senate seat left vacant by President Obama. Blagojevich's legal problems unfolded around the same time that Governor Paterson was deliberating on his choice to replace Clinton.

The political climate was murky for Paterson. He was dealing with a huge budget deficit and a bombardment of television commercials criticizing the way he was handling the crisis. Should the Governor pick someone to help him win over voters in upstate New York, or choose someone from New York City and risk alienating the upstate population? Choosing a male could jeopardize the female vote. Someone Hispanic could help him with Latinos. Paterson was caught in a quandary. His indecisiveness was widely viewed as a lack of leadership. The process blew up in his face.

Meanwhile, political mind games were afoot. Tedisco staffers jokingly took bets on who the new Junior Senator from New York would be. "I think Attorney General Andrew Cuomo gets it," one of them said. "No, I think the Governor needs to choose a woman," another replied. Cuomo, New York's Attorney General at the time, was also a good possibility for the post. Several polls had actually put him at the top of the list. Cuomo was enjoying high marks from New York voters. That's the nature of his post as Attorney General. They enforce the law. They bust bad people who commit awful deeds. To most people, it seems as though an Attorney General could do no wrong. It's the perfect job to gain the trust of the people. Plus, it didn't hurt that his father, Mario Cuomo, was a popular New York State Governor. The younger Cuomo had also been grabbing headlines for going after Wall Street greed. The previous State Attorney General, Eliot Spitzer, who built a reputation chasing down Wall Street crooks, was elected governor with a huge majority of the vote.

The slight possibility of Gillibrand getting the nod did cross Tedisco's mind. Her appointment to the Senate would open up New York's 20th Congressional District seat. Gillibrand had represented that district for a little over two years. She claimed it by beating out incumbent Republican Congressman John Sweeney in 2006 during one of the nastiest and most expensive congressional races in the country.[9] She had no chance against the better-known Sweeney, who gained national attention during the Florida recount in 2000. Sweeney had played a key role for President George W. Bush in the debacle. Mr. Bush later nicknamed him, "Congressman Kickass." But Gillibrand had an ace in the hole. Just days before the election, information leaked out about an emergency phone call made from Sweeney's house, allegedly by his wife. The police report claimed that Sweeney was knocking his wife around. The damage was done.

Gillibrand also had a decisive win over her Republican opponent in the 2008 elections. She was wildly popular in the District even though the majority of her constituents were considered to be highly conservative. She called herself a Blue Dog Democrat, which is a Democrat with conservative leanings. She also came from a family of Republicans. Some observers said that she was a political prostitute – someone who would do whatever it takes to win. Her job approval rating was at 70%+, according to local polls. She was comfortable and safe enough in her district to take on any challenger. She was a young, short, blond – an attractive woman with striking eyes and a bright smile. She was always well-dressed on television interviews. Simply put, she was the quintessential politician.

Tedisco's political instincts kicked into overdrive early. He had suspected that neither Cuomo nor Kennedy would get the appointment. Cuomo had become Governor Paterson's political adversary. The son of former Governor Mario Cuomo no doubt wanted to follow in his father's footsteps. To get there, he would have had to beat Paterson in a primary. Sources inside the governor's staff confirmed that the two men didn't really mesh well politically. As for Kennedy, Paterson was in a bind. Critics were tough on the daughter of Camelot. According to insiders, Paterson also thought that Kennedy was in over her head. Gillibrand was, more or less, the obvious choice.

Knowing the political inside game, Tedisco had started to carry himself differently, as if he was already running for Congress. He desperately wanted to turn the 20th Congressional District seat back into Republican hands in case Gillibrand became the new Senator from New York. His focus gradually shifted from the New York State Assembly to the 20th Congressional District. "I think I could win," he thought with measured confidence.

Tedisco had been critical of the process that Governor Paterson legally used to find Clinton's replacement. He had called for a special election, claiming that the decision to replace a U.S. senator was too important to be left in the hands of one person, namely himself. He wanted people to think that he believed candidates had to be vetted by the public and the only way to do that is through elections. "I'm sure Caroline Kennedy is a nice person, but no one knows where she stands on the issues," Tedisco said in press conferences. He was secretly hoping that Congresswoman Gillibrand would get the job to force a special election in her seat.

Kennedy shocked the political world and gave Tedisco hope for higher office when she decided to withdraw her name from consideration for the Senate. She generated the same media buzz as she did when she proclaimed her interest. She put out a brief statement that said, "I informed Governor Paterson today that for personal reasons, I am withdrawing my name from consideration for the United States Senate." Just like that, she called it quits, causing a political firestorm for Governor Paterson. Was Kennedy pushed out? Did she really leave because of personal reasons? There were conflicting reports that she bowed out gracefully after learning that Governor Paterson was not going to select her anyway.

Paterson had snubbed a powerful Kennedy. To make sure that he didn't take the blame, his office leaked private information about Kennedy's Senate run to make her look like a poor candidate.[10] Paterson denied that there had been a leak. However, the Senate search made him look incompetent, sloppy, and disorganized. Kennedy was handpicked by powers bigger than Governor Paterson. Insiders said that the requests and suggestions to select her to replace Clinton came from as high up as President Obama. Kennedy had helped Obama during his campaign. She gave Obama instant credibility with Kennedy family supporters. Paterson had essentially snubbed the President of the United States as well.

Gillibrand, who most New Yorkers barely knew, had become the frontrunner. New York Senator Charles Schumer greatly influenced the process. Schumer had been involved in New York politics since 1974. He was one of the most well-known and well-connected Democrats in the State until Clinton came along and stole a major part of the spotlight. Even as a Junior Senator, the former First Lady upstaged Schumer.[11] She had more star power and more connections than

Schumer could ever have. Gillibrand would bring balance to the power structure between the two New York senators. She would take her rightful place as a junior senator.

The shocking news came one day after Kennedy officially dropped out of the race. Governor Paterson had finally made up his mind and declared Gillibrand the new Senator. Many Democrats were not happy. Several members of New York's Congressional Delegation expressed their dissatisfaction with Governor Paterson's decision. He had picked an upstate conservative Democrat, turning the left wing of the party against him.

Gillibrand tried to do some damage control. The Blue Dog Democrat quickly changed her tune. She was endorsed by the National Rifle Association as a congresswoman. All of a sudden, as a senator, she was calling for changes in gun laws that the NRA would never support. The woman, who went against a proposal that would have given illegal immigrants driver's licenses in New York State, was supporting initiatives to give illegal immigrants easier access to a taxpayer funded college education. Gillibrand, who never supported same-sex marriage as a congresswoman, became strongly in favor of allowing same-sex couples to legally wed. Observers said that she had turned 180 degrees, like a political prostitute. Governor Paterson's approval rating then plummeted to one of the lowest in history.

With a weak Democratic governor, a bad economy after Democrats swept into power, and his superb name recognition, Tedisco knew he had all the right ingredients in place to mount a great congressional campaign. He was about to embark on an incredible journey. He felt that it was the right time to make a run for Congress.

The Urge to Run

J ames Tedisco's main office door at the New York State Capitol was shut tight. Out in the halls was the hustle and bustle of lobbyists and special interest groups chasing down their targeted politicians. Some of Tedisco's top staff was milling around in a room adjacent to the main office. They were awfully quiet with half-smiles on their faces, as if they knew something was about to go down, something no one else knew, something that could lead to big changes in the office. It was the kind of smile that made inquiring minds ask questions.

Secrets are not unusual in politics, even among people playing for the same team and fighting for the same exact cause. Sexual relationships were even more secretive. Staffers said it was pretty common for lawmakers to fool around with interns or their staff. Yet only a handful have been caught and punished. That was the culture at the State Capitol. Keep your mouth shut in the interest of job security, and the problems would fester. In fact, secrecy and loyalty often caused riffs among Tedisco's senior advisors. No one was sharing information – more so this time around than in the past. Tedisco's urge to run for Congress was perhaps one of the best-kept secrets at the State Capitol.

When the power meeting was over, Tedisco's main office door flung open. The staff slowly trickled out, staring at each other with eyes that told the story of things to come. There were those who knew and those who had a feeling about Tedisco's intentions to get involved in another election. It hadn't been that long since the last one. Just three months earlier, Tedisco and his 41 Republican colleagues in the New York State Assembly jumped into the political trenches to fight for their seats. Another campaign meant late nights, early mornings, and lots of coffee and doughnuts for Tedisco's staff. They hadn't had a break in years. There had been one special election after another before the general contest in November 2008. It seemed that they were always in election mode. They were certainly not looking forward to a congressional race, which is ten times bigger than that to which they were accustomed.

The staff also raised a lot of questions. Was it the right time for Tedisco? Had he thought this through? Eight years of President George W. Bush had made the political climate extremely difficult for Republicans. Bush's approval rating was in the toilet – one of the lowest in presidential history. Many Americans often spewed extreme and sometimes sharp rhetoric aimed at Mr. Bush. He was so toxic, some people even said they were not comfortable calling themselves Republicans.[12]

Many political observers drew parallels from the 1970's, when it became nearly impossible to elect Republicans because of the Watergate Scandal that brought down President Richard Nixon. Fast forward to 2008, the country was angry at Republicans once again. The fallout started in 2006 when Democrats took back the majority in Congress. Two years later, they increased that majority into a super majority in the Senate. Reversing that trend could prove to be a tall order for one small New York State lawmaker.

But Tedisco felt ready for the task. What could possibly go wrong anyway? He's a conservative in a conservative district. It's the perfect match. Political insiders assumed that the GOP had finally reached the bottom. There was nowhere else to go but up. The right candidate could churn up a comeback wave. Besides, all politics are local. It didn't matter that President Obama, after nearly two months in office, was still enjoying high marks nationwide, even from voters in New York's 20th Congressional District.

It didn't matter that Kirsten Gillibrand, a democrat, was extremely well-liked in that district. Tedisco was going for it. It was almost like a higher calling. "I believe people move public servants from one level to another," Tedisco always said whenever asked if he'd be interested in higher office. "Public servants can't actually make those decisions themselves," he would add.

Tedisco's interest in the 20th Congressional District didn't pop out of thin air. The longtime state lawmaker had been looking at that seat long before Governor Paterson officially named Kirsten Gillibrand as New York's new junior senator. He had to take a backseat in the late '90s for another candidate to run, according to Tedisco's own recollections. The seat had become vacant when veteran Republican Congressman Gerald Solomon retired. Salomon picked former Congressman John Sweeney as the party's standard-bearer to replace him. Tedisco also gave up another opportunity in 2008, "all for the good of my fellow Republicans," he said. That was the year when Kirsten Gillibrand defeated wealthy GE heir, Sandy Treadwell.

This time was different. After being patient and working for so long to help other Republicans get elected, Tedisco felt that his moment had arrived. After years of taking a backseat to watch others get ahead, he felt that his turn had finally come. His top aides believed, if nothing else, the party owed him that much, and the seat was a present for all of his hard work. "There's no way he could lose," they said. "Once he gets the nomination, it's a done deal. Tedisco is off to Washington," the staff added.

Tedisco had made a deal with the Republican members in the State Assembly that he would stay on as their leader during the anticipated short special election for Congress. The desired outcome was to make a smooth transition after the election from State Assemblyman to Congressman.

Every single one of Tedisco's top aides thought nothing could stand in their way. As far as they knew, they were already on a plane to Washington with Congressman Tedisco. They were celebrating in their hearts and mind. What could possibly go wrong?

"I don't see how the Democrats can get this seat back unless they come up with an unbelievable candidate. I'm not sure they have one of those candidates. I think they were stupid to appoint Gillibrand to the U.S. Senate," people said. Who could blame them? Tedisco seemed to be the right fit at the time. He had all the necessary credentials, or so it seemed. He was well-known and had never before lost an election.

The New York State Assembly's entire Republican conference felt the same way too. Many of them would prematurely congratulate Tedisco and called him Congressman. They would see him in the halls of the State Capitol, shake his hand, and treat him as if he was already a sitting congressman. Part of the reason for that was political survival. They were kissing his feet, hoping for something in return, like campaign cash or federal pork money, if and when Tedisco made it to Congress. Federal politicians usually have access to bigger pots of money than local officials.

From that point on, Tedisco was more careful around television cameras and reporters. He tried to appear stately instead of his usual aggressive, straight shooter self. He was stiff, restricted, and couldn't come up with decent ideas.

Tedisco just wasn't himself. It seemed as though his top advisor was pushing him to be someone else other than himself. Many reporters who followed Tedisco had a feeling that something was brewing. They always knew Tedisco would seek higher office. The proof was in a write-up in a New York City publication about Tedisco's possible candidacy for lieutenant governor with New York City Mayor Michael Bloomberg or former presidential candidate Rudi Giuliani at the top of the ticket for governor.

Somehow, lieutenant governor might have made more sense for the upstate New York Republican. He was extremely interested in that job. He frequently joked about what a wonderful ticket Giuliani and Tedisco would make. A Bloomberg and Tedisco team was not as attractive because he always thought the New York City Mayor was slightly too liberal. Tedisco didn't think he would have had enough support to run for governor, although, the thought of running for New York State did cross his mind from time to time.

Rumors about a possible run for statewide office created quite a buzz. He always thought a one-term governor would be the best way to solve the state's problems. "That governor would not be afraid of re-election which would allow him or her to make all the right decisions for the needs of the people instead of the needs and wants of special interest groups and politicians," Tedisco would say.

A politician's worst fear is perhaps the thought of not getting re-elected. That's why they seem to work so hard to stay in power. That's why they try to take credit publicly for everything possible in order to make sure that voters remember them instead of their opponents. A governor with plans of only serving out one term wouldn't have to worry about the reins of power. Only then would that governor be able to fix New York according to Tedisco.

After his many years in the New York State Assembly, Congress seemed like the next step and the best possible opportunity available for Tedisco. A run for governor or lieutenant governor was unlikely in his immediate future. Money is a good indicator in those situations. Money equals support. President Obama raised a lot more campaign cash than Senator McCain. That indicated that the American people were in the mood for change. They sent more money to the person who they thought would most likely bring about change.

Tedisco didn't have a lot of his own money, and he wasn't raising much either as a state lawmaker. Public support was not there. He was only 58 years old. He still had plenty of time left for something else to pop up. Politics is highly unpredictable. And as the saying goes, there's no better time like the present. Congress was obtainable right away.

The day had come to make his intentions public. The press was already fishing around the Capitol for answers.

Somehow, many of them already knew that Tedisco was going for it. His staff just couldn't keep a secret that long. Some key aides leaked the information to a few reporters.

Tedisco confirmed what they already knew. He was interested in the 20th Congressional District seat left vacant by Kirsten Gillibrand. It was exciting and exhilarating. Tedisco once again had fire in his belly and a big smile on his face. All he had to do was secure the nomination of the Republican Party.

Selecting a Candidate

Three or even four cell phones were not enough to handle the volume of calls coming in and out, inquiring about Jim Tedisco's bid to get the Republican Party's nomination for Congress. He was juggling his congressional campaign with his duties as New York State Assembly Minority Leader. Since he couldn't use state-funded phones at the State Capitol to make calls about the Congressional race, Tedisco's top aides used their private cell phones to manage the process.

There wasn't a moment in time when Tedisco didn't have a cell phone up to his ear trying to convince the big wigs of the Republican Party in the 20th Congressional District that he was the right candidate to take back the seat from the Democratic Party. This was not a time to be too aggressive. Tedisco was humble, carefully choosing his words to make his case. "Mr. Chairman, I would really appreciate your support to run for Congress," he said on the phone, with sincerity.

Since this was a special election, there was no time for a primary. The nomination process had to go through the political parties' county chairs, state leaders, and party elites, also known as the party bosses. They take a look at résumés, check backgrounds and talk to the candidates to guide their decision process. They then go into a little room and put their brains together to pick the best person. That's how it's done. The candidates have to almost beg to gain their support. If you make the party bosses feel important enough in the nomination procedure, then you might be considered seriously. The candidate with the most connections and who is owed the most favors usually gets the nod.

The 20th Congressional District had an open seat. It generated a lot of interest because vacant seats tend to be competitive and in-play for both major parties. It's widely known that incumbents are tough to beat. About 98% of them get re-elected in the New York State Legislature during any given election cycle. Congress is no different, coming in at a 90% rate of return. That trend is more popular today than in the early years of American politics.

Public office used to denote service for your country. In those days, members of Congress were not even paid a yearly salary. They used to receive a per diem while they were in session. Today, most elected officials see public service as a career with a sizable paycheck, and they rarely want to give it up. A member of Congress makes close to $180,000 a year. They can retire after 20 to 25 years of service, with up to 80% of their pay replaced. What's not to like? Political scholars say that politics has become a selfish business.

Most politicians care more about serving themselves than serving their country or community. Political neophytes have very little chance of winning against incumbents, an average of about two percent in New York. It's not a level playing field. Incumbents are well-known in their districts. They're at the spaghetti dinners, the chicken barbe-cue luncheons, and the parades. They also bring home the bacon. You may have noticed that earmarks, or funds that each district allots to their politicians, come pouring into your community around election time. Political insiders say that's no accident. It's a great way to remind and encourage voters to cast their ballot a certain way.

With an open field in the 20th Congressional District, the candidate pool had become a bit crowded. The party bosses' cell phones were ringing off the hook. Tedisco's first few phone calls were made in an effort to eliminate the competition. His two biggest obstacles were John Faso, a former Republican New York State Assemblyman who ran for governor, and Republican New York State Senator Betty Little.

When he got Faso on the phone, it wasn't pretty. "John, I just wanted to let you know that I'm throwing my hat in the ring for the 20th Congressional District, and I'd like to have your support," he told Faso in the short phone conversation. After a few more exchanges, Tedisco hung up and chuckled. Faso wasn't about to lend his support to his primary competitor. Instead, he hit the streets quickly with a fundraising campaign. He had also started to heavily promote himself as the apparent Republican frontrunner on the radio, in newspapers, and on the six o'clock news. That was the start of a big fight among New York State Republicans, which lasted throughout the campaign, and beyond the election.

Faso thought he would be the best candidate to face the Democrats. After all, he was the one who sacrificed himself for the Republican Party when he ran for governor against former Governor Eliot Spitzer and lost by one of the widest margins in history. He was the one who unsuccessfully ran for New York State Comptroller as a Republican and lost. He had given so much to his party; the nomination for Congress would have been his payback since the open seat was seen as a sure win for the Republicans.

It was much the same for Senator Little. It seemed that her bitterness grew stronger during the selection process. She would refuse to return phone calls from Tedisco. She had also started her own phone campaign to convince the party bosses that Tedisco would be a terrible choice and that a female candidate was the best possible chance that Republicans had to start making a comeback. Little, at the time, was the highest-ranking Republican woman in New York. She's a moderate, a position that many insiders believe would have played well in the 20th Congressional District.

The Republican trio butted heads in the press. Keep in mind that they were good friends before the 20th Congressional District race put a wedge between them. Tedisco, Faso, and Little had worked in unison in the past to try to elevate their party. They would often be spotted at the same events, speaking in order to convey a positive message for the Republicans. They were like family. But family, like any other relationship, can buckle under the weight of political disagreement. Tedisco, Faso, and Little wanted a Republican to win the race. But they disagreed on the identity of that Republican.[13]

Meanwhile, the party bosses met in secret to pick their favorite candidate. Right out of the gate, Tedisco had the biggest chunk of support. Saratoga County, which makes up more than 30% of New York's 20th Congressional District, was in the bag for Tedisco. The County Chair and other powerful players in the background all went to bat for Tedisco. It seemed like a *fait accompli* with that kind support. Saratoga County is sandwiched right in the middle of the District. Little's support came from the Northern portion of the District and Faso's was in the Southern counties. They couldn't come close to Tedisco's big lead.

The one reservation regarding Tedisco was that he didn't exactly live in the District. His primary residence was about four blocks away from the District line. Both Faso and Little were lifelong residents. They hammered at the residency issue and made sure that the media was fully aware of it. To them, Tedisco was an outsider trying to gain political power. The carpetbagger label was thrown around a few times, especially since upstate New Yorkers are picky about their roots. When former First Lady Hillary Clinton ran for the U.S. Senate to represent New York, she and her supporters fought hard to overcome the carpetbagger label. Clinton and her husband, the former president, moved to New York just before she ran for the seat. Robert Kennedy, the brother of former President John F. Kennedy, was also heavily criticized in the '60s when he tried to represent New York in the Senate, as he was from Massachusetts. Observers say that he won the seat by a slim margin because of his residency problem.[14]

Was Tedisco a real carpetbagger? He was running in a district in which he could not vote. "I can't believe they think I'm a carpetbagger. I've been here all my life," Tedisco said to reporters and critics who brought up the issue. Tedisco did represent parts of the 20th Congressional District as a state assemblyman. The Congressional District lines were different from the State Assembly lines. He and his wife also owned a home in the most populated county in the Congressional District. Tedisco had a legal right to run for the seat.

According to the U.S. Constitution, the congressional candidate has to be at least 25 years of age, a U.S. citizen for at least seven years, and live in the state of the Congressional District. They would, of course, face difficulty in trying to convince voters why they care about a community which they only visit on occasion. To the public at large, Tedisco was always known as the Assemblyman from Schenectady, a city outside the congressional district. That was where he went to high school and college. That's where he had his deepest roots. Many voters in Schenectady even tried to go to the polls on Election Day and were confused when they found out they couldn't vote for Tedisco for Congress. His residency problem became unnecessary baggage, but it wasn't enough to kill his support for the nomination.

On a cold winter day in January 2009, Tedisco and his top aides took a slow walk over to the front steps of the State Capitol. Along the way, congratulatory phone calls poured in from Republican Party bosses. Tedisco looked calm and sure of himself. He didn't flinch nor fidget. He had a smile on his face while his most trusted advisors leaned over to clue him in on what to say to the press.

On the front steps of the Capitol, a slew of television cameras and reporters were lined up, waiting for the person they thought was already on his way to Washington, D.C. Tedisco walked towards the scrum. They met him halfway with reporters and photographers scrambling to get the best possible angle. "Being chosen as the standard bearer of the Republican Party is an honor, a privilege, and a critical first step on this journey," Tedisco said to start off his prepared remarks. That was his very first press conference after receiving word that he had won the Republican nomination for Congress.

That was the day on which many people thought Tedisco had become the new congressman. His top aides were so confident that they were already trying to figure out what jobs would go to whom in Tedisco's new congressional office. "Who will travel with Tedisco to Washington every Monday?" a top advisor asked. "Everyone will have options. You can either stay with the state or go work for the feds," others would say. As the old saying goes, never count your chickens before they hatch.

The Democratic Party had a different vision of the future. It was one where Tedisco wasn't even a state lawmaker, let alone a congressman. They knew that he was a fierce competitor and one of their biggest critics. "Oh, God forbid he becomes a congressman," one Democrat said in an elevator. It's interesting how much you can learn in elevator conversations. People said vile things about Tedisco without knowing who was listening. Perhaps they didn't care who was listening. Maybe they wanted Tedisco to know how they felt about him. "I can't stand the man, but he's going to win anyway," another woman said. A two-minute elevator ride in the New York State Assembly often revealed how personal party politics had become. The two sides really hated each other, all because of power, jobs, and money.

While many Democratic leaders also thought Tedisco would win, the party was still collecting applications from possible candidates. Their process was the same as the Republicans. There was no primary. The party-bosses had to work together to pick the best possible candidate. Scott Murphy was among dozens of hopefuls who wanted to represent New York's 20th Congressional District.[15] The name of a former local television news anchor was tossed around as the frontrunner. "We will crucify her in the election. What does she know about politics? She was just a stupid anchor," some of Tedisco's aides said of the journalist. A news anchor has name recognition, the kind that could match, or even surpass, Tedisco's. Most people in the District didn't know Murphy or how serious the Democrats were considering his candidacy. His name barely came up in hypothetical conversations as a possible challenger.

Tedisco had a head start on the Democrats. But that didn't give him any real advantage. Faso and Little, both Republicans, were furious that they were denied a shot at the contest. GOP power brokers had rushed the nomination process. Insiders say it was rigged from the start – Little and Faso never even had a chance to make their case. Even if Tedisco was the right candidate, his party was not 100% behind him. The GOP was divided, and supporters of Faso and Little were not shy about expressing their dissatisfaction with Tedisco. The blogs were on fire with Republican criticism. They said Tedisco was the wrong candidate, running at the wrong time, surrounded by the wrong people in the wrong congressional district. They also predicted that Tedisco would lose.

The Republican Party was already falling apart nationally. Their in-fighting in this all-important race for GOP survival was only making things worse. The Democrats had done it right, it seemed. They slowly went through the nomination process to select a candidate that the entire Democratic Party would back. Even though party insiders had some reservations about Murphy, they didn't feel like the process was rigged.[16]

As the first official candidate, Tedisco was out campaigning one week before the Democratic nominee emerged. He held his first rally called Women for Tedisco, in anticipation that the Democrats would pick a woman to run against him. For the Republicans, all signs were pointing to a wealthy female challenger. The campaign was trying to soften Tedisco's image early to counteract the combative and aggressive reputation that he had garnered in government for more than two decades. The campaign quickly abandoned the Women for Tedisco movement as soon as it found out that the Democrats were going in a different direction.

The Democrats met on Super Bowl Sunday to pick their nominee. The field was narrowed down to just a handful of candidates including Scott Murphy. The Tedisco campaign was enjoying the big game when news broke out that Murphy had won the nomination. "Scott who?" was the biggest question of the night. Most Americans were glued to the television set to watch the Pittsburgh

Steelers and the Arizona Cardinals in action. But at that moment for Tedisco, Murphy had become more interesting. "I heard he's putting in hundreds of thousands of his own money. I still think we'll crush him," one Tedisco's aides said. "He doesn't have any name recognition at all. I think the Democrats would have been better off with the former news anchor," another aide said gleefully. The confidence level among the Tedisco team was now through the roof.

Murphy was a Harvard graduate, a self-made millionaire venture capitalist from Missouri who moved to the District three years before he decided to run for public office. He was not seen as an outsider mainly because his wife had a large extended family and deep roots in the District. One of Murphy's biggest assets was that he came to the table with hundreds of thousands of dollars of his own money. The Democratic Party had found a candidate who would, at the very least, be competitive with his own money.[17]

Building a Message

The New York State Republican headquarters was a three-story, historic brownstone located in the heart of downtown Albany, NY. Inside, the 19th century architecture was preserved after years of renovations. Pictures of past Republican leaders, like Governor Nelson Rockefeller, graced the walls where the receptionist welcomed guests. The original wooden floors and stairs were so old that they still creaked and squeaked with every single step, even after the restorations.

The tall staircase that graced the foyer corkscrewed all the way up to the third floor. That's where New York State Assembly Republicans made their political home. It was a familiar spot where Tedisco and his aides hashed out plans of attack. There was something uncomfortable about the old, three-room office space. The hallways were narrow. The carpeted areas were dark and dirty. There was paperwork scattered everywhere on the tables, desks, and shelves.

Since Tedisco had not yet set up his headquarters for the congressional campaign, the Old State Assembly political office temporarily served that purpose. Tedisco's aides would set up appointments to meet prospective vendors and consultants for the race. Several campaign television commercial producers made their way up the creaky stairs to present their ideas and plan of action for Tedisco. But it was one phone conversation in the old office that would set the tone for the first few weeks of the campaign.

Tedisco always got emotional when he spoke of his family and the events that shaped his life. He grew up in a blue-collar home. His father was a foundry worker at General Electric in Schenectady for 40 years. Foundry employees worked with molten metal and heavy machinery. "In those days, the foundry was hell on earth, a rough place to make a living," Tedisco said to the political commercial producer. This was supposed to be a quick hello, an initial contact with a vendor. But the conversation stretched into a touchy, soul-searching discussion that even made some of Tedisco's staff uncomfortable. "My father was a hard worker. He never complained," Tedisco added.

One day, when he was suspended from school for causing trouble, the elder Tedisco took his son to the foundry. The young Tedisco remembered seeing an orange glow and heat ripples rising from the molten metal. Black soot rained down on employees who were hard at work, wearing their hard hats, gloves, and other protective gear as they shoveled coal into a furnace. Sweat poured down their faces from controlling heavy machinery. The air was thick and unbearable. Tedisco said that he sat there at a young age and watched his father work the entire shift in the most atrocious conditions. At the end of the day, his father took him in the locker room where they changed into their normal street clothes. "In the locker room, my father taught me something else. He said blow your nose son," Tedisco said with tears streaming down his face. "Blow your nose son," he added, overcome with emotion. His staff was stunned. They had never seen that side of Tedisco before. The commercial producer was also speechless. "That's powerful stuff," were the only words he could muster.

There was more to the story. Tedisco said he wasn't the best student when he was a teenager. His father also took the opportunity (in the locker room) to address this. When he finally blew his nose, thick black soot came out. His father said, "Son, you can come down here and work with me, or you can work hard, go to school, and make something of yourself." As Tedisco told the story, you could see each word taking an emotional toll.

With great difficulty, Tedisco recalled the family tragedy of his brother's untimely death. His younger brother, Joey, was born with Down Syndrome and died at the age of 15. He recalled the family sacrificing everything to take care of little Joey. He said his little brother's illness dominated the family life. Every decision they made was centered on little Joey. The conversation finally wound down, and Tedisco was an emotional wreck. Some of his deepest and most poignant feelings had found their way to the surface. That was exactly the kind of material that the producer needed in order to craft a message and reintroduce Tedisco to the public for Congress.

Not many people had previously heard Tedisco vocalize these thoughts. A significant portion of his staff was completely unaware. The public certainly didn't know this side of Tedisco. Few people knew that he was a special education teacher and guidance counselor. Nor was it common knowledge that Tedisco coached basketball. He was mostly known as a basketball legend from Schenectady, NY, who came from the same streets as Pat Riley, one of the greatest professional basketball coaches of all time. Riley served as head coach for five championship teams in the NBA, including Miami Heat and Los Angeles Lakers, before retiring in 2008. Both Tedisco and Riley shot hoops and worked at basketball summer camps together back in the 1970s. Tedisco was only 5 feet and 7 inches tall, but he could dunk a basketball. "I walked around with weights attached to my ankles for a year," Tedisco said of his ability to reach the basketball rim. He was an all-American and the all-time leading scorer at Union College in Schenectady, NY.

In his New York State Assembly office, evidence of his basketball career was everywhere. There were pictures, framed newspaper clippings, signed basketballs, trophies, and awards. One particular photograph that stood out was a shot of a young Tedisco, with his yellow basketball uniform from Union College, shooting a jumper during a game. Years later, in his late 50s, he could still make that same hoop although it's slightly sluggish.

The public servant, Tedisco, also made a name for himself as a fighter, a lawmaker who called it straight. He was the loyal opposition – a kind of watchdog in the New York State Legislature. His claim to national prominence in politics came about when he opposed former New York Governor Eliot Spitzer from giving driver's licenses to illegal immigrants. The little known Republican Minority Leader of the State Assembly picked a fight with Spitzer, who was elected by a landslide. With only 41 Republican members out of 150 in the State Assembly, Tedisco didn't have enough votes on his side of the aisle to oppose Spitzer's plan. So he took his fight to the airwaves, proclaiming that Spitzer's idea to give illegal immigrants driver's licenses was dangerous.

The plan made national news when the late Tim Russert from NBC News asked presidential candidate Hillary Clinton, during a debate, if she supported driver's licenses for illegal immigrants. Clinton wouldn't answer the question. Tedisco was live on CNN and other news networks, trying to rally enough support to kill the plan. According to many polls, the American public did agree with him. Spitzer had to scrub his proposal after tremendous pressure.

The two men had their disagreements before. Spitzer is a Democrat, and Tedisco is a Republican. With two different philosophies, it's hard to maintain a working relationship without heated discourse. But following an exchange that made national news, their dynamic escalated to a different level. They were having a conversation about a press conference. When Tedisco refused to commit his presence, Spitzer threw a major fit. "He said, 'I'm a [(insert "f" word here)] steamroller, and I will roll all over you,'" Tedisco explained.

Then in early March 2008, news broke in the New York Times that Governor Spitzer, who gained national fame for keeping Wall Street in check as New York State Attorney General, was implicated in a prostitution ring. He was caught on federal wiretap, setting up trysts with high-priced hookers. The news sent shockwaves across New York State and across the country. All work at the State Capitol came to a screeching halt. People were glued to their office television sets in disbelief.

Tedisco and his Republican colleagues in the State Assembly were in the middle of a conference when they found out. Their smart phones went off one-by-one, alerting them of the breaking news on Internet blogs. Out in the halls of the Capitol, they went, mingling with others who were walking around without a purpose. They were all thinking in unison. Was what they saw and just read on the news actually true?

It didn't take long for the cameras to find Tedisco. He was always flexible and available for the press, especially television news. He loved to be on the news. Reporters could call Tedisco on a Sunday morning, and they'd be able to get a response. His initial response on Spitzer's prostitution problem was timid for an aggressive guy like Tedisco. "Better safe than sorry," he said to his top aides. He didn't have enough information then to launch an attack.

Later that afternoon, Spitzer appeared on national television with a brief message to the people of New York. "Today, I want to briefly address a private matter. I've acted in a way that violates my obligation to my family," Spitzer said in his prepared statement. Spitzer's apparent admission to being a John was all Tedisco needed to put a target on the disgraced governor's head. National news trucks set up camp outside the State Capitol, giving Americans a soap opera-like coverage of the story. The media savvy Tedisco made sure that he was part of the headlines. He quickly called for Spitzer's resignation. He threatened articles of impeachment if Spitzer had refused to resign on his own. He was the only lawmaker in New York who was pressuring Spitzer to quit. Radio hosts, like Sean Hannity and Glenn Beck, ate it up. For a short time, Tedisco became a regular face and voice on the airwaves. Even people in Africa said they spotted Tedisco on television news, according to an e-mail that came into Tedisco's assembly office. Spitzer's demise had gone worldwide.

The media circus ended two days later when Spitzer called a press conference to resign. The man who was supposed to be on his way to the White House, the sheriff of Wall Street, had crashed and burned. It wouldn't be fair to say that Tedisco loved the fact that Spitzer ruined his own career. He didn't enjoy seeing the destruction. But simply playing a role in its immediate aftermath paid him dividends. He had become more popular than ever for cashing in on the downfall of a once powerful governor.

That's the kind of Tedisco with whom the public was familiar for more than two decades. The Tedisco they knew was a bulldog. The Tedisco with whom they were familiar had a nose for issues that could resonate with the masses. The Assemblyman they knew had the kind of political instincts that had worked for him for the past 26 years in government. His softer side had never been tested. However, Tedisco's account of his family history and the events that shaped his life were so moving to the campaign team that they were convinced that there was no way they could lose with a story that was so deeply human.

Meanwhile, his opponent, Scott Murphy, was working on his own human story to introduce himself to the voters of New York's 20th Congressional District. He was an absolute unknown, a blank slate. His background had started to make its way around the blogs on the Internet. He grew up in Columbia, Missouri and moved to the District three years before he jumped into the race. Published reports revealed that the people closest to him thought he was aiming for local politics – a mayor or council member – when he said he was interested in running for office.[18] He was brand new to politics, unless you count his time as an aide to two Democratic governors in Missouri. But Murphy used his biggest assets to start off his campaign – his massive extended family. He told voters that he was a family man with a 60-second commercial, featuring his wife and three children. He also bragged about spending every Sunday with his children and dozens of his extended relatives who have deep ties in the District. The message was simple. It created the idea that Murphy was a human being to whom the average person could relate.

To set himself apart from Tedisco, Murphy used his lack of political experience as a positive, much like Barack Obama did when he ran for president. The plan, it seemed, was to paint Tedisco as an old and out of touch career politician. In contrast, Murphy sold himself as a successful businessman, a millionaire venture capitalist – a fresh face who could solve problems in Washington.

Then there was President Obama and the Democratic Party enjoying high marks from voters. Obama was on top of the world. Murphy didn't waste a second without aligning himself with the popular president. It was a different story for Republicans. At the time, the party had no clear leadership or message. It seemed that the GOP was imploding. It was the perfect combination for Murphy and the perfect storm for Tedisco.

Both men remained positive for a short time. Tedisco's first ad about his family history and his time as a teacher and guidance counselor drew some criticism. Many people thought he was wrong to use his little brother's disability and death in a political ad. [The commercial also dubbed Tedisco as "one of us." In other words, he was a native of the local community. That set-up only magnified Tedisco's residency problem. He didn't live in the district. Murphy did, and his wife's strong ties to the area would offset the fact that he was only a three-year resident of the district.]

Internal polling put Tedisco right out front with a 22-point lead. But going negative was always part of the plan. As the saying goes among insiders in politics, you have to define your opponent to the voters before they define themselves. For the Tedisco camp, Murphy was a tough one to attack. He had no public record and no controversial votes from which to draw. They couldn't go after his family. That would have been too personal. The only possible target was Murphy's business background and his lack of experience in public service.

With the stroke of a pen, President Obama threw the first curve ball in the battle between Tedisco and Murphy. The president signed the American Recovery and Reinvestment Act of 2009, also known as the Stimulus Package.[19] In the wake of an economic downturn, the act provided $787 billion to stimulate the American economy. The measure was an effort to create and/or save jobs by investing in tax relief, infrastructure, education, health-care and the energy industry. The stimulus package also included other spending which was largely criticized by Republicans as waste. Murphy quickly embraced the plan, saying that he would have voted up on the bill had he been a Congressman. Tedisco refused to give a straight answer when asked by the press.

This was the same Tedisco who always called it like he saw it. This was the same Assemblyman who never minced words even when going against some of the most power-ful elements at the New York State Legislature. This was the same boisterous assemblyman who called for Governor Spitzer's resignation. He rarely found himself in a situation where he couldn't make a comment. Finally, as a congres-sional candidate, when it mattered the most in his entire career, the straight talker was avoiding a question. "This is a 1,100 page document. I know there are some good parts in it and some bad parts," Tedisco said to the press. "What happened to Tedisco? Why can't he give us a straight an-swer anymore?" reporters asked. "He's looking really bad right now," they added. Tedisco's lack of a response to the stimulus package played right into Murphy's message that Tedisco was just another career politician who dodges questions.

The topic dominated the race for weeks. Murphy took full advantage of it. He called on Tedisco to take a stand on the stimulus plan everyday while singing the praises of President Obama. His camp would arm the press with exact questions designed to force Tedisco to answer. It's not like Tedisco didn't want to answer the question. His instincts were good. A succinct response would put the topic to bed, he thought to himself. He would have joined the ranks of Congressional Republicans who voted no on the stimulus bill anyway. Like many Americans, mostly Conservatives, Tedisco thought that the U.S. was borrowing too much money in order to stimulate the economy. "When you have money problems, going into debt will not solve it. You're just pushing the problem onto future generations," he would say.

The entire nation was also suffering from taxpayer spending fatigue. President Bush, before he left office, approved a multi-billion dollar plan to bailout crumbling financial institutions. The Obama administration was involved in dolling out oodles of public money to financial houses as well. For some people, there was no distinction between the bailout and the stimulus package. The bank bailout rescued banks. The stimulus package was meant to create jobs and cut taxes. Tedisco knew the country needed a boost but he didn't think the stimulus package as signed by the President, was quite the right medicine. Staying neutral was a campaign decision.

Tedisco's camp looked at poll numbers and noticed that voters in New York's 20th Congressional District were split on the stimulus package. Supporting the measure would put him at odds with Congressional Republicans. Rejecting it would open up a whole new can of worms. New York State had a big slice of the money, more than $20 billion of the $787 billion plan. The campaign thought Murphy would have quickly produced a television ad saying that Tedisco was against federal funding for education and infrastructure for New York. The staff was torn on whether or not Tedisco should give a straight answer. The campaign turned into a power struggle between Tedisco's local aides and a crew from both the National Republican Campaign Committee and the Republican National Committee out of Washington, DC.

What seemed clear was that Tedisco didn't make any solid decision without first clearing it with William Sherman, his chief of staff from the New York State Assembly – his most trusted advisor. Sherman played a major role when Tedisco tried to become leader of the Republicans in the State Assembly. At the time Tedisco was just another state sssemblyman. The leadership position elevated his political career. That's how Sherman was able to secure the job of Chief of Staff. Tedisco's promotion brought Sherman from a mid-level position in that organization to the top job. Think of it as if Tedisco was the CEO of the Assembly Republicans and Sherman was the COO, the Chief Operating Officer. Aides who had been with Tedisco for two decades felt slighted and say that's why Tedisco was obligated to listen and trust everything that Sherman had to say.

The strategy was to avoid the stimulus question at all cost, stay neutral when cornered and accuse the press of partisan politics for bringing up the topic. Meanwhile, the clock was ticking. Election Day was just a few weeks away and Tedisco stuck to his message. The fight within the campaign was at a boiling point. Things went awry when a new independent poll showed Tedisco's big 21-point lead was down to just four points. The veteran Republican felt that he had to do something to change the momentum. He held a press conference to say that Washington, DC was no longer in charge and that he was taking over full responsibility of the campaign.

"Those individuals out in Washington understand government and politics, but they don't understand the people of the 20th Congressional District as well as I think and the people who are on my staff and I do," he told the press. The staff from Washington was furious. They were caught unaware of Tedisco's new strategy to blame them for campaign problems. Tedisco's local campaign staff had been running the race all along. Nothing was done unless it was approved by Tedisco's top advisor Bill Sherman.

When Tedisco finally decided to clear up the confusion of how he would have voted on the stimulus bill, American International Group, AIG, was in the midst of a huge mess. Many Americans were outraged that AIG had given bonuses to its executives after taking huge sums of taxpayer dollars to bail them out. The company was on the brink of collapsing because of the massive downturn in the U.S. economy partly blamed on their bad investments.[20] Tedisco seized this opportunity, to try to reverse Murphy's momentum both as a New York State government official and as a candidate.

Inside the State Capitol, a few members of the press gathered to hear what Tedisco and his Assembly Republican Conference had to say about AIG. Since Assembly Republicans had very little power in New York, reporters were seldom interested in attending their press events. That day, they had a greater turnout than ever expected. Tedisco made the stunning revelation, in a long-winded statement that he would have voted against the stimulus bill had he been a congressman. "Here's the answer folks, get ready... NO!" he said in dramatic fashion. Within minutes, it seemed Murphy's camp produced a television ad saying Tedisco would have voted against President Obama's stimulus plan to turn the U.S. economy around including the largest tax cut in American history.

For those who knew Tedisco, he was back to his old self - the watchdog Assemblyman who wasn't afraid to be blunt. But the tides were seemingly against him already. Murphy had aligned himself with the extremely popular President Obama. His popularity and name recognition was on the rise. Many voters saw a smooth, young and fairly good-looking candidate in Murphy. In addition, Tedisco's campaign had admittedly recognized some of its mistakes.

To answer or not to answer the question of how he would have voted on the stimulus package had become a gigantic error. It didn't show up in the polls as a problem. However, Murphy's ads calling Tedisco a typical career politician had begun to resonate with some voters. His refusal to answer yes or no on the stimulus package reinforced the label.

Things were looking bleak when Tedisco's fortune suddenly boosted. The stimulus package that threw the first curve ball in the election, added another twist. The plan had a provision to cap executive bonuses for companies bailed out of financial ruin with billions of tax dollars. But the language excluded bonuses agreed upon in contracts prior to the passage of the stimulus bill in February 2009.[21]

The furor over AIG grew stronger. The anger was also redirected toward U.S. lawmakers who had rushed the bill through Congress and admitted that they didn't read the bill and, therefore, didn't know about the provision.The tables were suddenly turned. Tedisco's refusal to take a vote on the stimulus bill became an almost instant asset instead of a liability. He told the press that the reason why it took him so long to take a stand was because he was trying to read the 1,100 page stimulus bill. "I read every bill that comes before me in the state legislature. I think it's the responsible thing to do on behalf of the people," Tedisco stated in his releases to the press. Tedisco had not personally read the stimulus bill. His lawyer did and thoroughly briefed him, which was the way such things usually worked. Both he and his lawyer said the bill was loaded with earmarks. He said that Murphy was irresponsible for embracing a bill he had never read.

It was now Murphy's turn to dodge questions. Did he read the stimulus bill that was in controversy with AIG executive bonuses? Tedisco never missed an opportunity to call on Murphy to answer that question. The last televised debates between the two candidates were mostly about the stimulus bill. Tedisco would bring up the issue after every question. Murphy would avoid answering it.

Was it too late for Tedisco? Well, it obviously was. Insiders say the damage had already been done. There was not enough time to reverse the momentum for a win. Tedisco's campaign message had gone through too many transformations others thought. There was no theme. The story about his father and the death of his brother had disappeared. There was only a back and forth barrage of attack ad after attack ad. What was seen as a sure win for Tedisco in the beginning had turned into an uphill battle and the possibility of a loss. The campaign knew it. Their internal poll numbers had Tedisco trailing Murphy by six percentage points.

The District and Redistricting

From far away, it looked like a compliment for President Barack Obama, a kind of bright bumper sticker from a fan. The red pick-up truck was a little beat up, sitting in the parking lot at the local fire department in Pleasant Valley, NY. The bumper sticker wasn't the official blue Obama campaign logo with the sun rising. Rather, it was red white and blue and spelled out the president's last name in the form of an acronym, O.B.Λ.M.Λ. But as you took a closer look, there was something else written underneath the commander in chief's name. The letters made up the phrase "One Big Ass Mistake America."

Just across the street, there was another car with the actual Obama campaign bumper sticker. In a small town like Pleasant Valley, a close-knit community, these political expressions didn't go unnoticed. One resident said the divide had been building slowly and steadily between life long locals and transplants from New York City. Those with deep roots in the community tend to be more conservative.

The academics such as professors, students and those who come up from The Big Apple tend to be more liberal. Observers point to that as the reality of the situation on the ground in parts of New York's 20th Congressional District.

The sprawling district occupies more than seven thousand square miles in the Eastern portion of Upstate New York. It is about seven times bigger than the state of Rhode Island with half the population and even fewer job opportunities and industry than the Ocean State. The district includes ten counties, mostly farms and rolling hills with a population of more than six hundred thousand people. The four to five-hour drive it takes to go from the south end to the northern most point of the district reveals sprinkles of city and suburban life.

The district map looked like a funky cowboy boot. That's the way the districts were drawn in New York. Each political party carved out its own nook and cranny to guarantee winnable elections. Those electoral geographic boundaries are redrawn every ten years by law. The process is called redistricting. It's done in response to U.S. Census data. People often move around every ten years and redistricting equalizes the population within district lines to make sure that all representatives have the same amount of constituents.

Politicians, guided by their own self-interest, conduct the process. The dominant party usually comes out on top. Recognizing the role of partisan politics, some states have taken the redistricting process completely out of the hands of elected officials – replacing them with an independent and bipartisan commission. In New York where partisan politics plays a major role, the district lines were so gerrymandered that neighbors right next door or across the street from each other often had different representatives. People not tuned in to the political world were easily confused as to which candidate to support.

"I'm pretty sure that I'm in your district. Last year I couldn't vote for Tonko. I'll vote for your guy this time," one woman said to a Tedisco staffer. The woman lives right on the district line that cuts through the middle of her town. Congressman Paul Tonko was the representative from New York's 21st district, which borders the 20th. The confusion happens because parts of Tonko's district line cross the Hudson River to carve out bits of Democratic strongholds in areas that clearly should be in the 20th Congressional District. The jagged edges that separate the two districts didn't make any sense other than the possibility that they were drawn with political motivation.

Tedisco's congressional career could be short-lived as many observers pointed out. Since Democrats had full control of New York State government, the 20th Congressional District could become a target for heavy redistricting. New York State has been steadily losing population, and that means house seats will be taken away through a process called reapportionment. New York went from more than 40 representatives in the 1940's to 29 in 2009 because of population loss. Experts predict that New York will continue to lose representation. The theory was that if Tedisco won, Democrats would merge portions of his district to neighboring districts forcing him to face off with another Republican or a solid Democrat for re-election.

But that was only a theory. Tedisco first had to win. Planning campaign stops was a nightmare for the Tedisco team in a district so vast. It was impossible to visit all four corners of the district in a short period of time. The team divided the area into three regions – the North, the South and the middle. The bulk of Tedisco's time was spent garnering support in the middle section where the majority of the electorate lived. That was the area where Tedisco's name recognition was strong. He knew that was his bread and butter spot.

The majority of voters in New York's 20th District are considered to be highly conservative. Republican politicians dominated the district for 28 years. In 2004, President George W. Bush won that district by eight points. Republicans out numbered Democrats by more than 70 thousand according to 2009 voter registrations. It was all a plus for the Tedisco campaign. There are some minor cultural differences. The district is 94% White. African Americans and Hispanics only made up about four percent. Farmers have an important role in the community and possess some political influence. Second Amendment rights activists are also a key voting block. Many residents take their hunting very seriously. For them the right to bear arms was not negotiable.

These gun owners had a tough time deciding which candidate to support. Murphy had a perfect score on the National Rifle Association exam for political candidates. The NRA rates politicians on their support for gun rights with a thorough written exam. The non-partisan organization also takes a look at a politician's legislative votes pertaining to gun ownership for the overall score. As a so-called Blue Dog Democrat, Murphy claimed to be a big supporter of the Second Amendment. Tedisco had a slightly lower score on the NRA test. He had a voting record on gun legislations from his 26 years as a State Assemblyman he could not hide. He also promoted himself as a big ally to gun owners. Still, Murphy had a perfect score and that was very attractive to gun owners in the district.

Keep in mind that this is the same district that voted for President Obama, a Democrat who's hardly a favorite among conservatives, especially after he was recorded at a private fundraiser in California that they were clinging to their guns and religion.[22] Mr. Obama was referring to the hope and loss of jobs for small town residents in Pennsylvania. This is the same district that voted for Senators Charles Schumer and Hillary Clinton, both strong gun control activists. The district's former congresswoman, Kirsten Gillibrand, was also a favorite among gun owners. She morphed into a gun control lawmaker after her appointment to the U.S. Senate.[23]

So are the majority of voters in the 20th Congressional District in New York really conservative? Well, that's debatable. It was historically GOP territory. Republicans dominated the district since the 1970's. The idea that an ultra conservative district, which is rare in the Northeast, would turn Democrat was unbelievable. Even when Tedisco was down in an independent poll by four percentage points, most voters in the district thought he couldn't lose because he was a popular Republican in a Republican district.[24]   Perhaps some New Yorkers are still living too much in the past. All indications point to a district that is splitting up.

New York State politics isn't hard to predict. It's considered a blue state. Democrats usually do better than Republicans. The biggest slice of the Democratic Party in the state is concentrated in New York City and its suburbs. Republicans always did better in Upstate New York, especially in the rural areas like the 20th District. But that's where the political winds may be shifting and elections are harder to predict. Democrats are gaining popularity and are winning the hearts of upstate voters. They took control of the State Senate in 2008. The upper house was in Republican hands since 1965.

Many local races that should have been a sure thing for Republicans turned into hard fought battles between the two parties. Sure you can blame some of it on the unpopular President George W. Bush. Insiders say they're not sure if New York Republicans will regain significant power when the pendulum swings back their way because voter attitudes toward the GOP have changed. In addition, analysts believe that Republican candidates in a blue state like New York are so afraid, they just try to blend in with the Democrats. Many of them run campaigns based on conservative principles like smaller government and low taxes, but they renege on those promises once elected.

Gone are the days when you could just slap an "R" in front of your name as a politician and expect it to carry any significant weight anywhere in upstate New York. Many voters are simply fed up and turned off by New York State politics as a whole. Some folks who were registered with a party didn't want to admit it on the campaign trail. Others identified themselves as Independents. The bottom line is that many parts of upstate New York should no longer be classified as Republican stronghold regardless of what voter registrations might suggest. There's no question that Conservatives still have a strong presence in upstate New York, but their voices are getting drowned out by progress from the left.

Then there's the new generation of Republicans, many of whom are not impressed with the politics of President Ronald Reagan, one of the most respected and successful conservative presidents in United States history. Young Republicans are more moderate than their parents and grandparents – a plus for candidate Murphy.

They often clash with the conservative wing of the party mainly on social issues. Gay marriage may be the biggest example. New York State struggled with the idea of allowing same-sex couples to legally wed. Driving through the 20th Congressional District, you'll find plenty of Democrats and Republicans against it. The youth is where the mindset drastically changes. "Hey I grew up in a Republican household," a campaign worker said during a visit in the Southern portion of the district. "I registered Republican because that's what everyone did in my house. I could care less if gay people get married," he added shrugging his shoulders.

Many young moderates in the district wanted a more progressive approach from the GOP. They believe that the religious right and extreme radicals have kidnapped the party, and they feel that they don't belong anymore. Some called themselves Obama Republicans. They didn't necessarily agree with the president completely; however, they simply liked him. They weren't ready to demonize the popular president yet. Conservatives believed that was the wrong direction for the party. Some have even dropped the Republican label. They say Republicans are losing because they've abandoned their roots. They've been watered down.

Tedisco was the ultimate conservative. He also believed that the GOP was falling apart because the party had moved away from its conservative principles. "We should have a big tent for the moderates. That's fine. I think Rudy

Giuliani is a great leader," he said of the former New York City Mayor. "But Giuliani still stands for the core principles of the Republican Party – low taxes and smaller government," he added. Tedisco often pointed to President Bush as a true conservative who was steamrolled in Washington. As Texas Governor, Mr. Bush held the line on spending and taxes. But as president, he spent too much, borrowed too much and left the country in debt. "Those are not the actions of a true conservative," he said.

Tedisco certainly had his work cut out for him. Republicans nationwide were in trouble with no clear leadership or direction. The district he had sought to represent was changing, turning more or less into a toss-up electorate according to political observers. His campaign may have been a little too confident. They went into the contest thinking it was their race to lose when in reality it might have been Tedisco who needed to change voters' attitudes. It might have been Tedisco, the conservative Republican, who needed to show the district that he was different from the rest of the Republican Party.

The Challenge of Raising Money

I f Jim Tedisco was not on the phone handling media interviews, he was in all likelihood asking voters and business owners for money. In the car and on the way to some kind of campaign event was no time to relax. With the contact list in hand, Tedisco and the staff members who usually tagged along were making calls, each one using their private cell phones to contact potential donors. Tedisco would finish a conversation with one cell phone, then someone else who might be interested in contributing to his campaign was on hold for him on another phone.

Part of the reason for the haste was that Tedisco had a short window to find enough money for his campaign. The job of politicians, unless they're rich enough to fund their own campaign, is to constantly beg for money. The begging is more intense during campaign season. For a special election like New York's 20th Congressional District, the intensity was unmanageable because the candidates were challenged to raise millions of dollars in about a month and without enough funding, Tedisco's candidacy would have been mediocre at best. The most important part of any successful campaign is cash flow. Free press comes second believe it or not. Making the news cycle is always a major priority. Most politicians love to get their faces on TV and their names in the newspapers. The free publicity is priceless.

The reality is that money wins elections in American politics.[25] Campaign finance laws have a lot of restrictions but those restrictions seem to make it easier for the rich to run for office. (More on that later). Candidates with the biggest war chess or the largest wad of cash, usually emerge victorious. Although, that's not always the case. There are exceptions to every rule. In 2008, the winner was outspent by the loser in more than two-dozen House of Representatives races across the country.[26]

On the other hand, President Obama beat Senator John McCain nearly two-to-one in fundraising during the 2008 presidential election. He had an obscene amount of money and large sums are now more important than ever because political elections have become a multi-billion dollar industry in the United States. Campaign commercials cost a lot of money. The producers can charge hundreds of thousands of dollars to produce them. Then add in the cost of flyers, campaign signs, websites, staff, campaign travel, etc., and you could spend inordinate sums of money.

Raising enough funds for a campaign can be quite a challenge, even if a candidate plans well. You need to find the "true believers" who are willing to dig into their pocketbooks to support your cause. Tedisco's fundraising team was filled with true believers who lived for the cause. They were "drinking the Kool Aid," as the political expression goes. They got involved because they felt that Tedisco and the Republican Party stood for something worthwhile and actually wanted to help the American people. This was their moment to make a difference. All political parties have true believers. Unfortunately, as many Americans have discovered, the business of politics can also be dirty and selfish.

In order to raise money, candidates must also bring something to the table to entice donors to write a check. "House Speaker Nancy Pelosi will not go gentle into the night. The Democrats will spend big bucks to defend this seat. We need another voice in Washington," Tedisco often said to the people willing to listen to his pitch for cash. He had the same basic message tailored for every prospective donor. Business owners would get the "tax and spend" rhetoric. "We need to lower taxes on our businesses. We need someone in Washington to put a stop to all the spending taking place. I'll stand up to Nancy Pelosi," Tedisco said.

Who's Nancy Pelosi? Most people in the 20th Congressional District probably had never even heard of her. House Speaker Pelosi was three breaths away from the presidency. The first female Speaker of the House, who represented the 8th Congressional District in California, was third in line should anything happen to the president and the vice president. Tedisco couldn't bash President Obama. It was much too soon after Obama's big celebration into office. Pelosi and the other house Democrats were fair game. Tedisco tried to use them as reasons why Washington needed change and why he was the best candidate to bring about change in Capitol Hill.

Political donations are not a tax write-off. It's a tough sell if the candidate has nothing to offer back. Tedisco would be a freshman representative in the minority in Congress. A freshman has no power even as a member of the majority. What could he possibly offer donors other than the hope that if elected, he would begin the process of turning the fortunes of the GOP around? Murphy, on the other hand, would be joining the majority in Congress. He pointed to the fact that he would be working side-by-side with other powerful Democrats like newly elected President Obama and New York's senior U.S. Senator Charles Schumer to make sure New York gets a fair shake in Washington. That was certainly an easier, more positive sell. Tedisco was playing on fears that the Democrats had become too powerful in Washington and that a one party rule is bad for the country.

Both candidates needed more than $1.5 million to mount a good fight in the 20th Congressional District. It seemed downright impossible, especially for a candidate like Tedisco and his team. He wasn't wealthy. Funding his campaign out of pocket was completely out of the question. His team had never raised this kind of money before in such a short period of time. This was a special election scheduled to take place within two months. However, they did have something going for them. The congressional seat had historically been in the hands of conservatives and Republicans.

The majority of voters, even Democrats, thought Tedisco would win. Plus, national Republicans were heavily involved early in the race, including the likes of former House Speaker Newt Gingrich who made a national plea for Tedisco. Gingrich is credited for leading a revolution in the House of Representatives that put Republicans back in the majority in the mid 1990's after 40 years of Democratic rule. Republicans across the country were pumped, desperate, and longing for an era like the mid-'90s when they were on top. That's why money for Tedisco's campaign came flowing in from people all over the country. Most of it came from the true believers in the Republican Party.

Wherever Tedisco went on the campaign trail, he was tracking down philanthropists. The goal was to have every donor max out. Because of campaign finance laws, individual donors rich, or poor, could only contribute $2,400 at the most to a federal candidate in 2009. Couples could give $4,800 – not a whole lot of money when you're trying to raise millions in one month. Most contributors don't max out either. Some donate less than a hundred bucks. Good luck turning those donations into millions.

For Scott Murphy, the task of finding cash to defend New York's 20th Congressional District for the Democrats was somewhat different. He had to first convince donors he was a viable candidate. The political newcomer loaned himself hundreds of thousands of dollars to get the ball rolling.[27]

Many contributors were waiting on the sidelines to see if his campaign would gain any traction before jumping in. The labor unions that ended up endorsing Murphy were very quiet in the beginning of the race. "I don't think this guy has a shot. But I think he might put up a respectable fight," one union leader said in confidence. The game changer for them came after the first independent poll showed Murphy gaining on Tedisco. Murphy's 21-point deficit early in the race had gone down to 12 points.[28] That was traction enough for the unions. They saw an opportunity for Democrats to retain the seat. They jumped in with a boat load of cash to help Murphy.[29]

It's still up for debate how much power the labor movement really had in changing voter attitudes toward Murphy or Tedisco. Overall, unions are shrinking across the country, both in the private and in the public sectors. The truth is that unions made up only 12% of the workforce in 2008, according to the U.S. Department of Labor. That's a far cry from 1983 when labor unions made up 20% of the workforce.[30] The biggest drop took place in the private sector. Theoretically, New York has one of the strongest union movements in the U.S. They seem to have incredible power in political races.. They have a lot of money and a large amount of manpower. Getting their endorsement doesn't guarantee a win. New York Republicans sometimes lose with or without union backing, and they can win with or without union endorsement as well. Candidates on both sides of the isle bend over backwards to get the labor movement behind them. The resources that they bring to the table are mind-boggling.

To give you an idea, the health care workers' union, 1199 SEIU, in New York, spent more than a half a million dollars alone on Murphy's behalf during the campaign, according to federal campaign filings. The union spent more money than the Democratic Congressional Campaign Committee on the House race. The expense included radio and television advertising and flyers to help Murphy's campaign in order to spread the voting message get his message out to the voters. The unions also had boots on the ground during the final stretch of Murphy's campaign in order to spread the voting message. Tedisco did get some third-party money, but nothing from labor unions.

The National Republican Trust PAC, a little known political group, poured nearly a million dollars into the race for Tedisco. The group ran commercials to try to turn voters against Murphy. Our Country Deserve Better PAC also chipped in more than $150,000 to help the Republican veteran with ads on both television and radio.

As to their personal fundraising efforts, the two rivals kept the same pace for the first few weeks of the race. There was nothing too controversial. Then there was the fight over President Obama's economic stimulus package. Murphy skipped ahead of the fundraising war, and the polls tightened up. Political expert James Carville said in his book, *40 More Years: How Democrats Will Rule The Next Generation*, that money doesn't lie. Polls lie because people lie. But he said the money always goes to the candidate with the biggest support[31] That's why President Obama was breaking so many fundraising records. The country was ready for a change, and Senator John McCain wasn't seen as an agent of change. Murphy's support was gaining steam and according to Carville's theory, that's why he was raising more money than Tedisco. Murphy had raised his profile, and some people started believing that he could actually pull this off.

Murphy had a little bit of an advantage over Tedisco. His party was in full control of New York State and the federal government. Democrats held every statewide office and controlled both Houses at the State Capitol in New York at the time of the election. Observers say it's hard to beat the party in control in fundraising. First of all, the Democrats had a well-oiled machine set up, especially in New York City where they have complete dominance. Tedisco's New York State Assembly staff often talked about patronage jobs in all levels of government in New York translated to big money for a party. Some of those workers are silently obligated to make donations almost like union dues. They give money to keep the machine in place in order to keep their jobs. Many people change party affiliation against their own philosophy in order to be considered for government jobs. Once you have a political machine, it's hard to break it down. It's much the same where Republicans dominate. Campaign money flows from patronage workers and their friends for job security.

Political action groups tend to donate more money to the majority party as well. When Republicans were in charge of the New York State Senate, the labor unions and lobbyists representing a wide spectrum of causes and organizations showered them with money. The party in power can promise the donors more in return. Then add a dash of President Obama, a mega star at the time, into the mix, and you have a winning combination for Murphy.

The Democratic candidate could tap into a wide range of popular politicians for money. He had Senator Charles Schumer and newly appointed Senator Kirsten Gillibrand at his disposal. Former President Bill Clinton and his wife Hillary were also fundraising attractions for Murphy, especially since New Yorkers love the Clintons so much. Even the unpopular New York Governor David Paterson brought people together to raise money for the newcomer. Murphy's fund raising was the "Who's Who" in American Politics.

Tedisco's campaign, on the other hand, lacked star power. Senator John McCain had just lost the presidential race against President Obama. How much help could he be? Governor Sarah Palin perhaps could have been a big help to the campaign. One trip to New York for Tedisco could have raised a good amount of money. She was extremely popular, and she was able to draw a crowd wherever she went. But Palin came with her own baggage. She turned into a polarizing figure. Observers believe the former Alaska Governor would have made it worse for Tedisco.

She was damaged goods after losing the election as McCain's vice presidential pick. Even some Republicans inside Tedisco's campaign thought she was too much to swallow. Former Massachusetts Governor Mitt Romney would have been exceptional. However, his involvement in the campaign was minimal at best. Besides, he was looking ahead to the next presidential election. He had no time for Tedisco, it seems. Former Arkansas Governor Mike Huckabee was never thought of by the campaign as a major attraction for fundraising.

Sean Hannity and Rush Limbaugh appeared to have been the most influential leaders of the Republican Party during the special election. They were the ones, as talk show hosts, who shouted the loudest and drove the conservative message home. They had a large and loyal audience. Tedisco's campaign avoided using the national talk shows throughout most of the race. The two radio personalities could have been extremely influential in fund raising. They would have gotten the conservative wing of the party more excited about Tedisco. But Limbaugh and Hannity are too divisive, especially for a candidate like Tedisco who was trying to appeal to independent voters in the congressional race. Democrats knew it. They even sent out mailers with pictures of Tedisco and Limbaugh next to each other, trying to draw the conclusion that both men were one in the same.

Tedisco got into some trouble when he talked about Limbaugh in a newspaper article. His quote was somewhat taken out of context. The paper asked Tedisco during an editorial board meeting what he thought about Rush Limbaugh. Tedisco said "the only constituents I'm worried about are the people in the 20th Congressional District. Rush Limbaugh is meaningless to me." He didn't disavow Limbaugh per se. He simply meant that he was concentrating on the constituents of the district instead of a talk show host. Tedisco was not a huge Limbaugh listener, but he respected the high-octane conservative radio figure for his work and success. The quote created trouble for him and conservatives. Hundreds called Tedisco's headquarters, claiming that they were angry and no longer supporting the Republican candidate because of his comment about Limbaugh.

The money was still coming in for Tedisco regardless of how much star power the Republican Party had or how angry the conservatives were because of the Limbaugh issue. Tedisco still had former House Speaker Gingrich at his corner. He still had former Presidential candidates Mitt Romney and Rudy Giuliani stumping for him from time to time. Plus, his campaign team had a list of motivated donors with extremely deep pockets. He had billionaires and multi-millionaires on the list to which money was no object.

One construction business owner in the 20th District told Tedisco "when you get to Congress to make sure you stand up against Card Check," during a meeting with the candidate. That was the only way Tedisco would have acquired his support along with a sizable donation check. Card Check was known formally as the Employee Free Choice Act. The measure allows unions to organize without the use of a secret ballot vote. If more than 50% of the employees sign cards, the secret ballot election is automatically waved and a union is formed. Under the old system, employers had the choice to voluntarily wave the secret ballot process and accept the union. Critics said that the bill was pay back from President Obama and and the Democrats who received strong support from the labor unions during the 2008 presidential election.

The business community didn't like the idea because it would take power away from them and dictated what goes on in their private businesses. Those who supported Card Check believed that businesses had been taking advantage of employees for years and that it was time they share the success of their companies with the middle class. Tedisco was against Card Check anyway. Voting it down was an easy promise to the business owner. In contrast, Scott Murphy fully supported Card Check. The issue was pretty much evenly divided within party lines. Most Democrats loved it while Republicans thought the measure took too much power away from businesses.

Perhaps the most impressive aspect of Tedisco's campaign was the way he used technology to raise money. President Obama was the first politician to successfully use the Internet to make money for his campaign. Obama had a strong following, a core group of staunch believers in his message of hope and change. A good chunk of Mr. Obama's war chess was built on small donations of $10 to $20 by millions of donors over the Internet. It was unprecedented. Tedisco's message wasn't strong, and he was not an international figure.

The Republicans still managed to raise hundreds of thousands of dollars with a cyber campaign he called 20 for 20. It was ground breaking for a congressional race. Tedisco called upon small donors on Youtube, Facebook and other social media websites to contribute $20 for New York's 20th Congressional District. Newt Gingrich even mentioned 20 for 20 during one of his speaking engagements. For many people, it was a lot easier to write a check for $20 than for a hundred. If you asked someone for $100 in one shot, chances are that you will not get the money. But if you asked that same lender for $20 every two weeks, you're getting the same amount over time without the sticker shock. That was the theory that drove Tedisco's online efforts helping his team to raise a bundle with just a few clicks of the mouse.

On the Campaign Trail

Newly elected Republican Party Chairman Michael Steele took a long trip to Albany, NY to meet with his candidate Jim Tedisco. He was taller than he looked on television. It's usually the other way around. People tend to look taller on television than they do in person. Steele had broad shoulders and stood like a retired basketball player. The two men met for a pow wow inside the old state Republican headquarters in downtown Albany. They talked about the special election and laid out a plan of action to win the 20th Congressional District race. This was Steele's first election as the national leader of the Republicans. He was in it to win it and make a name for himself. "That win will send a powerful signal to the rest of the country, especially those folks in the elite media who think they know more than the rest of us. Our game is not up. Our message still rings true with countless Americans, specifically those in the 20th District," Steele said.

The GOP picked Steele to turn the party around after massive election losses across the country in 2006 and 2008. The new leader felt the need to come and greet his first candidate face-to-face as a way to kick off the campaign. He believed that Tedisco could be the candidate to right the GOP ship. It was the perfect opportunity. A seemingly conservative seat suddenly opened up, and a conservative and well-known candidate, like Tedisco, went after it. This race was winnable, and Steele would have taken credit for it behind the scenes, nationally, should Tedisco come out on top. He had a lot riding on the outcome.

Steele looked intimidating because of his stature. Some Tedisco staffers were excited to see their party's new leader in the flesh. He was a new face. He brought new hope to a party that seemed to be spiraling into extinction. Other Tedisco aides were skeptical about what Steele could do to restore the Grand Old Party. "He's been a good politician and a charismatic speaker but I'm not sure he's a good manager. The chairman needs to be a great manager," the aides said. They weren't pleased with the way he was elected chairman. The process was dramatic and took six ballots to put Steele at the top. He was the GOP's first African-American leader.[32] Insiders said that the part chose him to make up for their lack of diversity. The country had just elected the first African - American President, who happened to be a Democrat. Steele might have been the GOP's way of reaching out to the black community and beginning to address its image problem.

The fact is, that the GOP was devoid of diversity. The party of Lincoln, it was no more. President Abraham Lincoln would probably not recognize his GOP today. The party used to embrace diversity. Edward Brooke, the first African-American Senator from Massachusetts was a Republican. In fact, all black members of Congress in the old days were all Republicans. Today, the majority of minorities, including most women serving in Congress, are Democrats.[33] It's been a stunning role reversal for the two parties in the past 100 years.

If you saw the Democratic Convention and the Republican Convention in 2008, you'd think they were taking place in two different countries. The purpose of a convention is to select the party's nominee for president. In the case of the Democrats, convention voters were nominating Barack Obama. The Republicans were casting their votes for Mr. McCain. Were it not for the English language being spoken at both events, the casual observer probably saw two different cultures. The Democrats clearly took the gold medal for diversity as some political insiders on television pointed out. A quick camera shot of the audience revealed what could have been a meeting at the United Nations. Some critics on 24-hour cable news exclaimed the GOP must have hated those panning audience shots at its convention where the majority of the audience was white.

The convention wasn't the only venue. At GOP events from New York City to the far North and far West of Upstate New York, there were always very few minorities in the room. The two or three out of more than hundreds who showed up, would often stick together thereby magnifying the situation. It looked like a good GOP move to bring in Steele. Many political experts believed that something had to be done in order for the GOP to change its image with minority groups.

Steele's presence in Albany was to set Tedisco's race in motion. The campaign started out with a bang. The veteran Republican was up in the polls – beating his opponent, Scott Murphy, by 21 points. But it was way too early. Voters weren't even plugged into the race yet. The survey was also misleading because at the time Murphy's name was a mystery. Nonetheless, Steele did mention to reporters that the race wouldn't be an easy win.

The Democrats were still having a good year. Behind closed doors though, he was happy that his horse was way ahead from the beginning. He had promised to dump some money into the race if Tedisco did his fair share in the fundraising efforts. His personal staff was in place, both in the district and back in Washington, cranking out press releases and plotting a course for victory. The plan was to thoroughly visit every county in the district at least once, no matter what. The trouble was that the district was so vast; visiting all four corners was unrealistic in a short election.

But with the blessing of his party chairman, Tedisco was off to meet the people of the 20th Congressional District.

Diners and politics go hand in hand -- kind of like apple pie and vanilla ice cream. They seem to be the perfect venue for politicians to shake hands with the people who are likely to go to the polls and vote for them. On any given day, Murphy and Tedisco could be found snaking their way through a diner in the district. In fact, there can't be a campaign without some kind of diner involved in America. President Barack Obama and Senator John McCain certainly spent a lot of time in small town diners across the country while on the campaign trail in 2008.[34] You couldn't turn on your television to watch the nightly news without seeing Obama or McCain enriching the lives of senior citizens by drinking soup at some main street diner in small town USA.

New York's 20th Congressional District is an array of small towns. So you can imagine that diners are fairly common. Scott Murphy and Jim Tedisco's campaign teams probably knew them all. There was one or two in almost every small town in the district. Down time during the campaign was often spent at diners. Nearly every campaign stop had to incorporate a diner. They're great political spots, perhaps due to the ease with which a candidate can slip in and out of them and shake hundreds of hands in a matter of minutes.

For the campaign team, it was torture to go in and out of diners, and smell all the food on a it was torture to go in and out of diners, and smell all the food on a hungry stomach without taking a bite.

First of all, the campaign was not glamorous for either Tedisco or his team. Then again, there's no such thing as glamour on the campaign trail, especially for short elections. It's bad food, long hours, sleepless nights and senseless banter with people you may not even like. If you want a good diet and to lose weight fast, join a campaign team. Tedisco and some of his aides lost dozens of pounds without even trying. A couple of volunteers from Massachusetts were living out of their suitcases just to be a part of this campaign. It's the thrill and the possible reward in the end that makes it all worthwhile for many staffers. "I want revenge," one staffer said. He was a volunteer for the Republican candidate in the 20th Congressional District who lost to Kirsten Gillibrand in 2006. There are no two ways about it. There will be a winner and a loser, when it's all said and done. To the victor go the spoils, and to the volunteer goes the government job.

Then there's the candidate juggling multiple tasks in the car, on the plane, and at about a dozen stops a day. The campaign would start at dusk. Murphy and Tedisco would remain active late into the night, in an attempt to get an edge in the race. The campaign trail was probably worse for Tedisco who had worked out a deal with his members in the New York State Assembly to remain their minority leader. This was at a time when the state legislature was in session trying to pass a controversial budget. Tedisco's presence in the process was crucial and demanding. He was also part of a special election for Congress that required his attention 24 hours a day, with a staff that had never before conducted such an election. He was lucky to find enough time to sleep.

Of course, his staff would be right behind him to make sure he didn't miss a single beat. They kept tabs on the speeches, the talking points, the research, and the names of potentially important rally attendees. Staff members have their pulse on everything to make sure the candidate doesn't sound like an idiot. With lack of sleep and bad food, people are bound to make mistakes. One Murphy supporter said that he would show up at businesses where he was neither invited nor where his staff had scheduled meetings. Tedisco's top staff had commitment issues. They were all ready to go back to their state jobs after the election. Politics rarely worked that way. If the candidate loses, the staff gets squat. They go home with their tails between their legs, so to speak. But win or lose, Tedisco's top staff had jobs waiting for them. In essence, their livelihood didn't depend on this campaign.

Each part of the district had its own flavor. The Southern portion had more of a New York City suburb feel which made sense because it was closer to Manhattan. Had it not been for the rolling hills, the farms, the quiet life and the lack of cell phone service, a visitor might feel like he or she was still in New York City. Many residents and the transients brought their Brooklyn or Long Island accents with them, along with the culinary taste of the Big Apple. It wasn't hard to find great pizza and awesome sandwiches. But Tedisco was more or less a stranger in the South. "Who's this guy? He's running for Congress?" one man asked at a diner in Delhi, NY, a quaint little town located in the Southwest portion of the district.

It seemed that people there were more concerned with, and knew more about, New York City politics than what was going on in Upstate New York. So they didn't really know Tedisco's background and exactly from where he had come. It was an eye-opening experience to see how unrecognizable Tedisco's name was. That's why he would often use a member of the New York State Assembly Republicans who represents those areas in the South to introduce him at campaign events. To those residents, the name Scott Murphy and Jim Tedisco didn't ring any bells at all. Both men were on equal footing. The only difference was that Tedisco had political experience and Murphy had business experience.

It was much the same reception when Tedisco visited the Northern portion of the District. Lake Placid, home of the 1980 Winter Olympics, had never heard of Tedisco until the special election got underway. For a New York State politician who often made national news, there was an enormous amount of people in the state who had no clue who he was. His popularity was concentrated mainly in the center of the district where the media coverage at the State Capitol was intense and Tedisco was often quoted in the local newspapers and television news stations. Since this was a special election, Tedisco's strategy was to focus on his base – the area where he was already the strongest. There was very little time for anything else.

That is not to say that Tedisco ignored the North and the South, though, some residents felt he didn't pay enough attention to many Southern towns. A number of farmers in those areas expressed their discontent with the Tedisco Campaign. Many said he failed to show up at scheduled events. That was out of character for Tedisco. As the Assembly Minority Leader, he always made it a point to show up to everything, big or small. He had never missed a barbecue. He had never missed a parade. He would work late into the night, just to make sure he shook every last hand at a diner. However, he couldn't ignore his day job at the New York State Legislature. Failing to show up at scheduled meetings in the State Capitol or the chamber for a vote could have been used against him in the congressional campaign.

Critics would say that Tedisco didn't care about his constituents since he didn't bother to show up for a vote on one of the most important state budgets ever. The press was hot on his trail trying to figure out if he was neglecting his duties at the Capitol. The truth is there wasn't enough time in a 24-hour day to run a congressional campaign and participate in a major state legislative session.

The local issues were somewhat mundane. There were no natural disasters to talk about, no poor people in dire straights to visit, and nothing catastrophic that would transform the conversation in the campaign. Farmers were concerned about milk prices – hardly a pressing issue when the nation's economy was imploding. Gun owners had their mind set on the Second Amendment – barely a big story when Americans were losing their jobs. The national economy was paramount and effectively upstaged every single issue of concern in the District.

It seemed like Tedisco and Murphy were going through the motions of visiting county after county, city after city, and town after town with the same national message of how they would help to create jobs and fix the economy when they arrive in Washington. That's what people wanted to hear. You couldn't turn on your television set without seeing a news story about the Dow Jones Industrial tanking or how gloomy the job market had become. People were worried about their jobs and their ability to feed their families and keep their homes.

The unemployment was sharply increasing. More and more Americans found themselves at the unemployment office. The threat of a depression, like the one in the 1930's, seemed like a stark possibility. Everywhere Tedisco and Murphy went, they naturally touted their ability to create jobs and bring America back from misery. Tedisco claimed to have created three thousand jobs during his tenure at the New York State Legislature. Murphy had called himself Mr. Jobs at one point because of the way he apparently put hundreds of people to work. The two candidates drove their point home so much they had become the butt of many jokes. "The way they sound, these guys must have created all the jobs in Upstate New York," one voter said during a campaign stop in Saratoga Springs, NY.

The energy was always positive at each and every rally. The candidates rarely came across an unfriendly crowd. Murphy's rallies were filled with people who supported and would eventually vote for him. Tedisco's rallies were littered with Republican Party organizers who would never vote for Murphy.

Television Ads Galore

Stuffing envelopes, attending spaghetti dinners and campaign rallies, making phone calls and hoofing it door to door are considered the heartbeat of a political campaign. But the real battle is often fought in your mailbox and on your television set, especially in cases where the candidates have to reach a bigger chunk of the population. Good old-fashioned shoe-leather campaigning works well for local races. If you're running for mayor of a small city, population 20 thousand, you could possibly knock on every door to personally introduce yourself. But candidates vying for higher office would have to knock on thousands, if not millions of doors to meet potential voters – an impossible feat.

The Internet is slowly giving candidates more choices to reach voters. President Barack Obama was the first candidate to use this medium to its full potential in the 2008 election. Many experts point out that Mr. Obama changed politics forever with the use of the Internet.

He took advantage of Youtube, Facebook and every free social media tool at his disposal to advertise his message. Despite his ground breaking use of the Internet, television is still the fastest way to reach the masses. Both President Obama and Senator John McCain spent a significant portion of their campaign fortunes on television ads. According to 2006 numbers from PQ Media, nearly $2 billion went into political television ads. That number increased significantly in 2008.

Jim Tedisco and his team knew from the beginning that television ads would play a big role in the race. Going negative wasn't a question of if, but when. The philosophy is that -- you have to define your opponents before they can define themselves. Scott Murphy was brand new. He was undefined. "You have to tell voters what the difference is between you and the other candidate. You have to give them a reason to vote for you and against the other person," one top aide said during a discussion about negative advertising. Tedisco's aides also knew the opposing side would eventually play dirty because negativity is simply the norm in politics.[35] They remembered the battle between now Senator Kirsten Gillibrand and John Sweeney, the man President Bush nicknamed Congressman Kick Ass. That fight was one of the nastiest the country had ever seen in recent political history.

The two sides played nice initially. Murphy's very first ad introduced his entire family. The 60 second commercial showed his wife and three children packed in a minivan with Murphy's voice saying "Some say you can learn a lot about a person from their family. Well I'm Scott Murphy, and I'd like to introduce you to mine." The ad went on to say that Murphy's large extended family of 57 kids, cousins, aunts and uncles get together every week for Sunday dinner.

That caught the attention of the Tedisco campaign early on. It was effective, slick, well produced and Murphy seemed like a natural. It was tough not to like a guy who came across like the average Joe raising a photogenic family. The Tedisco campaign didn't think it was realistic for a family of 57 people to get together every Sunday for dinner. That was their only criticism of the commercial. However, they knew that Murphy could be trouble because it seemed like the political rookie was serious about mounting a challenging campaign based on his first ad.

Tedisco's first ad was also an explanation of exactly who he was. The ad started on a sad note about how Tedisco's little brother died of Down Syndrome. The woman voice-over ended the piece by saying "He fights for us because he's one of us." That line never got any real traction with voters. Tedisco had a residency problem. He didn't live in the district. The "one of us" line was supposed to soften the blow. But instead, that theme generated some negative feedback. Many people said that Tedisco should not have used his dead brother for political gains.

Others had no idea that Tedisco was a Special Ed teacher and a basketball coach and they'd promised to vote for him based on that. The one consensus among voters -- Tedisco's ad simply wasn't as slick and well produced as Murphy's. Many people also thought Tedisco looked angry in the piece. He wasn't himself. He looked like someone over directed him, turning the veteran politician into a robot. Tedisco was not used to reading scripts. He's the kind of politician who's better off-the-cuff. You can just wind him up and let him go. He'd come up with some of his best material impromptu right on a podium with half a dozen cameras pointing at him. Somehow the script for the commercial put Tedisco in a box. He looked uncomfortable and somewhat shy.

The gloves came off quickly in the special election. There was no time to waste. Tedisco and Murphy only had a month to make an impression before the polls opened. So, the love fest on television went on for a couple of weeks. Then, keeping their promise to take down Murphy before he even started, Tedisco's team threw the first punch. They came out swinging in an ad that questioned Murphy's assertion that he had created hundreds of jobs. The attack ad aired after the national GOP had already gone after Murphy by accusing him of tax evasion. The Republicans obtained paperwork that they claimed showed Murphy failing to pay taxes for one of the businesses he owned. Murphy said he'd paid all of his outstanding taxes.

The question still remains: why did the GOP make the first negative move? Negative political ads work, plain and simple. The sleazier they are, the better. The accusations can get personal and below the belt. Many political insiders believe Tedisco should have never even mentioned Murphy's name in any ad. He's a veteran politician who should have known better. Tedisco was running against an unknown. Many of his own aides said he could have run a totally positive campaign and completely ignored the fact that Murphy was his opponent. He also had the opportunity in this case to take the high road. But his team was bent on going negative.

Tedisco was skeptical about the strategy. He wanted to take a different approach after getting a lot of feedback from voters in the district. He was getting phone calls. Some people would stop him on the streets just to let him know they were displeased with the negativity. The Tedisco team had tunnel vision. They didn't want to hear anything other than their own ideas. They were confident that Tedisco could win regardless of who struck the first punch. Their next target was Murphy's success as a millionaire venture capitalist. Tedisco's commercials were now full of references calling Murphy a Wall Street Millionaire. They were trying to turn the businessman's success into a liability, which goes against everything Republicans believe in. When have Republicans ever criticized financial success?

It didn't take long, though, for Murphy to strike back with a few shots of his own. Murphy's negative ads were subtle. They were crafted in a way that made them seem like positive advertising. In many of them, Murphy would be smiling and the background music sounded almost comical. Murphy's main theme in his negative commercials pinned Tedisco as a typical Albany politician. Tedisco had been in government for more than two decades. It was a believable depiction of Tedisco, especially at a time when incumbents were not very popular with the masses. People were fed up with New York politicians. Those who paid attention would look for opportunities to take out incumbents. It didn't always work out that way. Incumbents always returned to office every two years despite the public's dissatisfaction. The reelection rate was at 98% (see Chapter 4).

Murphy never passed up an opportunity to mention President Obama's name in his commercials. He went out of his way to say how much he supported the president and his policies. The president was on cloud nine after winning the 2008 election against Senator John McCain. The country was still in love with Mr. Obama in March 2009 when Murphy and Tedisco faced off. After eight years of President George W. Bush, the electorate wanted nothing to do with Republicans. The 20th Congressional District in New York felt the same way. Obama's name was like gold on the rise and Murphy went along for the ride but he steered clear of New York Governor David Paterson.

He never once mentioned the governor's name in his ads. Paterson had some of the lowest approval ratings in history.

The airwaves heated up when President Obama signed the $700 billion stimulus bill into law. Murphy quickly came out in support of the law and the president. Tedisco's reluctance to take a stand on the issue created a home run topic for Murphy. Nearly every American knew about the stimulus package. It appeared at a time when many Americans were losing their jobs. They were also afraid of losing their homes and not having enough money to feed their families. The stimulus package was perhaps the only possible solution to make everything better. Murphy's campaign produced an ad criticizing Tedisco for his refusal to say whether he'd support President Obama and the stimulus package.

The Tedisco campaign didn't want to react to the stimulus attack that was quietly eroding his lead. The ad called Tedisco a typical New York politician who couldn't make a decision on one of the country's most important bills. Tedisco kept trying to deflect questions about the stimulus package from the press. The more he deflected, the more the ads against him made sense. People in the district were beginning to ask questions. They wanted to know why Tedisco couldn't do an ad of his own that would put the stimulus package issue to bed. "We can't do a commercial about the stimulus package. We want the issue to go away. That would magnify it," the Tedisco Campaign said. If you're explaining yourself, you're losing. That was another Tedisco campaign motto. Responding to the stimulus attack was not an option. Leave the issue alone and it will disappear. Except, the stimulus issue wasn't disappearing.

Many political experts point out negative ads can be effective. But they can also backfire or make the candidates taking the shots look desperate. Tedisco was the experienced politician. He didn't need to be desperate. He specifically asked his team to tone down the negativity, but no one listened. They argued against it even when polls showed that Tedisco's numbers were dwindling in the center portion of the district, they were holding steady or going up in the southern portion. All the negative ads were aired mostly in the center. Resident's in the southern part didn't see many negative messages from Tedisco. The campaign had its first evidence that their negativity was backfiring. [36]

The answer to Murphy's stimulus attack ads was more attack ads from the Tedisco campaign. They criticized Murphy for creating jobs in India instead of here in the U.S. The ad seemed to have had the opposite effect again. It elevated Murphy's profile as a job creator. Some people were willing to overlook the fact that the jobs went to a different country. Murphy fired back with another ad suggesting that the jobs in India made him enough profits to reinvest in creating jobs in the U.S. Murphy then tagged the ad with a memorable tongue-and-cheek comment, "Jim, what's wrong with that?"

At that point, television viewers were downright miffed by the barrage of political advertising on the air. You couldn't turn on your television without seeing a Murphy or Tedisco commercial. Nearly every commercial break in the evening news showed the candidates making their case. You'd see a news story about Murphy and Tedisco. Then seconds later, the first two commercials would feature, Murphy and Tedisco. They were the only game in town -- the only special election for a house seat in the country. Political hacks from across the nation were focused on the race. Both candidates had millions of dollars and only about a month to spend it all. It wasn't hard for them to capture everybody's attention.

The intensity of the campaign would turn up once more on the air when Tedisco said that he would not have voted for the stimulus package had he been in Congress. Then news broke that AIG, American International Group, a company that received government bailout money, gave out bonuses to its employees. It turned out that the stimulus bill had a clause buried in it that allowed companies to give out bonuses even though they had received bailout money. Murphy's ad said Tedisco was against stimulating the economy.

The Tedisco campaign said that Murphy supported bonuses for companies that taxpayers helped bail out. The commercials were coming out so fast from so many different factions and groups, that the Tedisco campaign couldn't keep up with them. Both men were throwing mud at each other in rapid successions. The National GOP and the National Democratic Party added to the hysteria with their own ads that were sometimes even more callous and insensitive.

Most of the ads from either side made outlandish claims that could be explained rationally. If you peeled back the layers of nonsense, both candidates would seem like people with whom you might consider having a beer with. But you would not know it by watching their commercials. According to the ads, Murphy was a Wall Street millionaire who could care less about the middle class, didn't like the U.S. Military, cheated on his taxes while bankrolling jobs in India and gave out bonuses to executives at companies losing millions of dollars.

As for Tedisco, the ads claimed that he was an old politician who cheated taxpayers out of money, lied about his record of job creation, voted against property tax relief, and helped his friends get high paying government jobs while accepting campaign cash from a convicted felon he helped. That was essentially the messages that both campaigns were trying to convey to the voters. Vote for me because the other guy is no good.

Independent groups, acting without candidate or party approval, seemed to have made things worse. Their ads were downright mean. Most of them tried to help Tedisco after sensing this was a competitive race. They saw Tedisco's poll numbers take a dive, and they wanted to make sure their conservative friend get a little boost.

"Our Country Deserves Better Pac" and the "National Republican Trust Pac" both produced commercials attacking Murphy. SEIU, Service Employees International Union went after Tedisco on Murphy's behalf when they realized that the newcomer could actually win. There were disclaimers at the end or the beginning of the commercials. Nobody pays close attention to those disclaimers anyway, except for party hacks. Regular viewers just see negativity. If it's directed at one candidate, they blame the other for it.

The two candidates and third parties hammered their point home on the air and in mailboxes. Residents in the 20th Congressional District were constantly bombarded with leaflets and full-color glossy cards with negative messages. One of them tried to link Tedisco with radio talk show host Rush Limbaugh, former President George W. Bush, and former Vice Presidential candidate Sara Palin. Murphy, on the other hand, tried to link himself with President Obama. The new president's picture was all over his mailers. Some of Tedisco's mailers brought up the jobs that Murphy created in India.

It was a hate fest; at least, that was the way some viewers saw it. The tone was so nasty, that many voters said they couldn't wait for the race to end. Both candidates were running positive, self-promoting ads simultaneously. They were drowned out by the onslaught of negative attacks. The Tedisco campaign tried to go back to the drawing board after an independent survey showed that the majority of voters viewed the GOP as the aggressor.[37]

The cameras came back on with Tedisco now delivering a subtle and uplifting message that focused on the economy and jobs. "In these difficult times, we're not Democrats or Republicans. We're Americans and that's the team I'm on," Tedisco said in the commercial to engage the independent voters in his closing argument. Why did people think Tedisco was more negative when both sides were rolling in mud? Some insiders say the candidate who launches the first attack is usually seen as more negative. The reality was that ads from the GOP, especially the ones from the national Republican congressional campaign team, looked and sounded more negative. The choice of music, voice-over and pictures contributed to what amounted to a playbook from old, dirty GOP politics.

The White House officially got involved in the race just days before voters went to the polls. Vice President Joe Biden was on the radio all over New York's 20th Congressional District making a final pitch on behalf of President Obama for Murphy. The ad gave Murphy instant credibility with voters. It touched on most of the issues Murphy and Tedisco fought over during the course of the campaign. "This is Vice President Joe Biden. As a graduate of Syracuse Law School, I not only root for the orange, I root for Upstate New York as well. That's why this special election you'll be holding next Tuesday, March 31st is so important to me. I'm supporting Scott Murphy for Congress, and so President Obama. Scott's a businessman who helped create over

1,000 jobs. He knows people have to work together to get things done, and he'll work with Democrats and Republicans in Congress to get things done for Upstate New York.

"That's why Scott supports our economic recovery plan, because it means 76,000 jobs for Upstate NY and funding for schools, which helps keep property taxes down. We have a lot of work to do, and Scott will help get it done. So I hope you'll vote next Tuesday. And I hope you'll join President Obama and me, Joe Biden, in supporting Scott Murphy. He's a businessman who knows how to create jobs for Upstate New York."

Phil Oliva, a longtime trusted Tedisco advisor said that the campaign had many missed opportunities. But he was cut out of the congressional campaign. Oliva said Tedisco should have never attacked Murphy. He should have left the negativity up to the independent groups and the National GOP. According to Olivia, perhaps one of the biggest mistakes was that the campaign ads never mentioned Tedisco's most popular legislative victory.

Tedisco was the original sponsor of the Buster's Bill. The law made aggravated cruelty to pets a felony. Animal lovers who happened to be Democrats said they would have voted for Tedisco based on Buster's Law. The animal protection message never quite made it out to the voters of the 20th Congressional District. Some in Tedisco's campaign team thought Buster's Law wasn't big enough to warrant a commercial. They thought that Tedisco had surpassed animal rights. He was too big a statesman to talk about animal abuse.

The Polls

You could hear the roar of the road noises inside campaign car as Tedisco and two aides were headed to yet another rally. The tension in the small sport utility vehicle was building. There was an urgent need to break the uncomfortable silence but no one wanted to utter the first word. Saying the wrong thing could mean trouble in a car with a few overtired and stressed out campaign workers. The candidate was in a zone after learning that poll numbers would be released in mere minutes. You could imagine a million questions running through his mind. How will I fair in the polls? Was it a good sample? What does it mean if my numbers go down?

Tedisco's nervous tick always pushed him to call his trusted advisor Bill Sherman. The calls would oftentimes make him feel better. Sherman didn't have the answers to the polls though. He could only encourage Tedisco to stay calm and that everything would be fine. This was different. Tedisco was running for Congress, the biggest and most important election of his life. His opponent, Scott Murphy, had made some gains in the last internal poll. This poll was more meaningful. More gains for Murphy would mean a negative trend for Tedisco. He had butterflies in his stomach, more now than ever before. Nothing but good numbers would settle his nerves at that point.

The cell phone rang. It was the moment of truth. The first independent poll had given Tedisco a 12-point lead over Scott Murphy.[38] There was no celebration or jubilation in the car. Tedisco and his aides were simply thankful to be ahead. A 12-point lead is better than being behind by 12 points. The campaign team was a little worried because Tedisco was ahead 21 points in a poll commissioned by his own campaign just a couple of weeks earlier. A nine-point drop was too much too soon. The Tedisco campaign did expect the numbers to tighten up. Their own poll had shown a dead heat in the 20th Congressional District when the candidates' names were omitted and the choice was between a Democrat and a Republican. Was it a sign for Tedisco to use a different campaign strategy? It seemed that voters were leaning toward a Democrat, any Democrat.

"I don't make decisions based on polls!" That is one of the most famous lines from politicians. They somehow want the public to think that their decisions are based on convictions and principles. For many of them, that couldn't be farther from the truth. Polls and scientific data are the driving force behind most decisions from your state house to the White House. These days, there's a poll for almost everything. The media and Americans as a whole seem to be fascinated with them. There are the usual same-sex marriage polls, the abortion polls and the death penalty polls. But you could also find numbers for what percentage of Americans prefers boxers over briefs or the amount of people in America who smoke pot or drink bottled water. Public opinion data seems to be everywhere and they matter a whole lot more to politicians, especially when the numbers could have a major impact on their career in public office.

The 20th Congressional District special election saw three independent polls in one month. There were countless other polls commissioned by the Democratic Party and the GOP. Think of them as sort of a crystal ball for candidates to be able to predict what the future holds or perhaps a report card of a politician's hard work. Every single poll was significant and made the chatter among Tedisco's aides more terrifying. "Did we get new numbers last night?" one aide would ask. "I don't think so. They're coming out tomorrow," another would reply. "What happens if our numbers go down," the whispers continued. "I don't think that would be a good trend. That would mean we could lose the race," a senior aide answered.

The second independent poll was highly anticipated by both sides as a possible game changer. The GOP's own internal polling at that point didn't yield positive results. Those numbers never made it out to the public. In that survey, Tedisco's campaign was bleeding profusely -- praying for better news from the independent data that would be released to the press. Any downward movement for Tedisco, even if he remained ahead, would kill his momentum. Murphy's people of course, hoping to shrink Tedisco's lead a little more. They also had to have internal data that gave them confidence.

The night before the release, a reliable source told Tedisco to brace himself for a major disappointment. Things didn't look good, for him at all. It was possibly one of the worst nights in the campaign. A slight dip might have been fine, easier on the stomach. Tedisco was looking at another sharp decline. The race was weeks away, but you could already hear a little bit of doubt and the feeling of possible defeat in his voice. For the first time, you could see fear in the eyes of the campaign manager and the rest of the senior campaign staff. It seemed possible that Tedisco could end up losing the race. "I'm not sure we can hang on to our lead," a senior staffer said. "It's possible we could lose this race," he continued.

The campaign team called a late meeting to figure out how to handle the press the following day. "How do we minimize the damage?" a senior campaign aide said on the conference call. They needed to change the subject quickly and steer reporters away from the poll numbers. Their plan was to tell the public the numbers didn't mean anything and they always knew this race would be a nail biter. They wanted to minimize the shock. Murphy's campaign, on the other hand, wanted "shock and awe." They wanted desperately to show how the newcomer was eroding a veteran politician's 21-point lead by leaps and bounds. The shocker finally hit early in the morning on radio and television that Tedisco was now leading by only four points.[39] How did this happen? How did a slick and well-known politician let a political neophyte get so close? How did Murphy manage to go from a 21-point deficit to the point where he might actually pull off an upset? People in the 20th Congressional District, Democrats and Republicans, were beside themselves. This can't be happening. The polls must be wrong.

Meanwhile, the Tedisco team was trying to manage the press but the damage was already done. Tedisco was no longer in the driver's seat of the election. It seemed as though Murphy was ahead when he was actually behind. Every story would say that Tedisco was in trouble instead of saying that he was still leading. What made things even worse, the poll's margin of error was 3.7%, only a fraction less than Tedisco's 4% lead. The race had essentially become a statistical dead heat. Panic started to set in. Tedisco needed to stop the bleeding. He needed something fast. During his first press conference, just hours after the independent poll, Tedisco blamed all campaign problems on the National GOP. He told the press he was now taking over the campaign. He wanted to relate directly to the people of the 20th Congressional District.

Some of the most important numbers in the surveys might have been overlooked by the Tedisco campaign. The data showed that Murphy's commercials were more effective. They were resonating with voters. A bigger percentage of people who saw Murphy's commercials were more likely to vote for him than the percentage of people who saw Tedisco's commercials. This was obviously a television fight. Some of Tedisco's top staff said that they should have hired a better commercial production team. But it was too late. With a signed contract, no matter how terrible the commercial, they were stuck.

Tedisco was also never above the 50% mark in any of the independent polls. His support remained in the 40's the whole time while Murphy's support kept increasing. In the first independent poll Tedisco was beating Murphy 46% to 34%. In the second one, Tedisco went down one point while Murphy jumped seven percentage points. The score was 45% Tedisco and 41% Murphy.

As the contest pushed ahead, internal poll numbers from the GOP were getting worse. "May be it's the stimulus package debate that's doing the damage," some Tedisco aides said. The GOP's own survey showed that the stimulus package was pretty much a 50/50 split in the 20th Congressional District between people who supported the measure and those who opposed it. Internal poll after internal poll had Tedisco going down from a four point lead into negative territory. The Republican pollster was hoping the numbers would magically go the other way. One even had Murphy leading by six percentage points. It was a sure sign for the campaign team that Tedisco might not be able to squeak this one out.

No one knew about the bad internal numbers, not even the candidate. The philosophy was: keep the candidate in the dark when he's losing. Bad poll numbers could demoralize any candidate and kill his or her motivation to push forward. Tedisco was now supposedly at the helm of his campaign, listening to his own instinct. He was making all the right moves again, according to many insiders. He had finally answered whether he'd vote for the stimulus Package that Murphy had supported from the beginning. He had produced new and more positive commercials to soften the negativity. He was back to being a fighter. He had found himself right where he usually was – fighting for a cause. He was fighting to keep his political career alive. He was fighting to turn the ship around.

Bad news from the polls would only turn him off. He knew he was in trouble. That's all he needed to know to re-invigorate his campaign. It was still tough for the campaign to remain positive. Polls, especially from trusted pollsters, are seen as scientific. They're usually not too far off except in certain extreme circumstances. Many pollsters don't trust their own polls when it comes to racial issues in America. People don't always express their true feelings about race. The person on the other end of the phone usually responds with a politically correct answer instead of what his or her true feelings. In 2008, Democrats were worried that they might not recapture the White House with a black candidate.

Even when Obama had a comfortable lead in the polls, some Democrats were nervous about the accuracy of the numbers. They thought people would pledge their support for Obama on the phone then vote the other way in the privacy of a voting booth. It's happened before. When Los Angeles Mayor Tom Bradley ran for California Governor in 1982, a last minute survey put him way ahead of his opponent. But the polls were wrong. Bradley, the black candidate, lost the race. The explanation, now known as the Bradley Effect, was that those who didn't want to appear racist told pollsters they would vote for Bradley.

However, behind the curtain in the voting booth, they cast their vote for the white candidate. Polls could be wrong even without race involved. Exit polls predicted Senator John Kerry would win the presidency against George W. Bush in 2004. This example also depends on whom you ask. For many Democrats, that exit poll was correct and Mr. Bush managed to steal the election. If you asked a Republican, they would say that the polls were wrong, and Democrats were sore losers. Political experts say that polls can be wrong for a variety of reasons. There could be a bad sample. The sample may also be too small. Some people may be under represented. Many households are also doing away with home phones.

Pollsters have to make up for cell phone users since they cannot call them. The answers may also depend on how the questions are asked. With the issue of race, for example, instead of asking people if they would vote for a black person, the pollster would phrase it as follows, "Do you think your neighbor would vote for a black president?" Some political scientists believe that this question gives a more accurate read on a person's feelings towards race. But there was no black and white issue in the 20th Congressional District race. Tedisco and Murphy were both white candidates in a district where nearly 95% of the voters were white.

President Obama had won the district with 51% of the votes in 2008. There was nothing controversial, no political correctness. Pollsters just couldn't get this one wrong. The questions were straightforward. You're either voting for Murphy or Tedisco. Nonetheless, the Tedisco team was hoping for a miracle. They were wishing for bad polling data. It was too late to turn anything around. The election was just about a week away.

The campaign team started to focus its attention on intensity. Republicans and Conservatives in the district were apparently hungrier for a win then Democrats, according to several polls. The campaign told the press their internal polling had put them ahead of Murphy and they were still expecting to win the race. That positive attitude was gone as soon as the television cameras and reporters disappeared. While Tedisco's campaign team hadn't given up yet, some were on the verge of calling it quits. Many Tedisco top staff had already tried to create opportunities for themselves elsewhere to make sure they had jobs after the election, especially his chief of staff from the State Assembly.

The third and last independent poll seemed to have been the final piece of the puzzle. It delivered a cold and depressing blow to the campaign. The cat was out of the bag quickly since bad news travels fast. Everyone became aware of what Tedisco's campaign team had known for more than a week after evaluating internal surveys. Tedisco was trailing Murphy by four percentage points.[40]

Again, Tedisco's support never made it out of the 40's. Murphy was beating him 47% to 43%. Apparently Tedisco also had a problem sealing the deal with Republicans. While Murphy had the support of nearly every Democrat in the district, only 64% of Republicans were supporting Tedisco. That was a low number in a district with more energized Republicans than Democrats. "Don't worry. The Republicans will come home and we'll win this race," some Tedisco aides said with their lips quivering. "Republicans always come home at the last minute. We'll get them," they added.

The national press had a field day with the new numbers. Their commentaries focused on the possible embarrassment for the National GOP with a Murphy victory. "If Republicans cannot win a seat that was handed to them on a silver platter, they really need to reevaluate their existence," one talk show host said.

The 20th Congressional District presumably belonged to the GOP. With more conservatives and Republicans, this race should be a slam-dunk. No one ever expected Tedisco to be behind in the polls. No one ever expected, despite New York Governor David Paterson's bad approval ratings that New York Democrats would still be in great shape.

It was a dagger in the heart for Tedisco when he learned that he was behind in the independent poll. He was on his way to breakfast early in the morning, but he had lost his appetite. He liked being an underdog but not at this stage of the game. The 26-year political veteran had never lost a race before. He didn't know what to make of it. This wasn't his race to lose. He was supposed to be in the lead. A conservative Republican shouldn't lose to a blue-dog Democrat in a Conservative district. What happened to all the Conservatives and the Republicans in the district? Perhaps it's true that the district was becoming more of a toss up? Why would they not want to support someone like Tedisco? Why would they want Murphy -- someone who admires President Barack Obama and all of his policies – to win? May be there weren't as many Republicans as the voter registration showed. Maybe the Tedisco campaign was way too negative. All those questions were swirling around the campaign. The numbers didn't make sense.

The survey even proved the numbers didn't make much sense because the majority of respondents in the poll still believed that Tedisco would win. That was pretty bizarre. Democrats and Republicans were convinced by a 45% to 35% margin that Murphy still had no chance.

Many political experts believed that Tedisco's campaign was poorly organized. There were many mistakes. The negative ads didn't seem to help. It wasn't Tedisco's best performance either. In a good year for Republicans, all those missteps and blunders wouldn't have mattered at all. In a bad year for the Republican Party, those missteps and blunders were magnified.

Take, for instance, the loss of a Republican stronghold in Mississippi. Democrat Travis Childers spanked Republican Greg Davis in a special election for Congress in May 2008. The district was in Republican hands for years. President George W. Bush won that same district three years earlier by a 62% margin against Senator John Kerry. The Republicans tried to link Childers to then presidential candidate Obama and the Reverend Jeremiah Wright controversy.

Reverend Wright had been Obama's pastor for years at his church in Chicago. Video of the pastor was all over the Internet and on national television damning the United States of America during a sermon at the church. The reverend also said in the video that the United States brought on the September 11th attacks with its own terrorism. Pastor Wright was so toxic, candidate Obama had to make a special speech about race relations while explaining his relationship with the Pastor.

Childers struck back with accusations that Republican Davis was linked to the Ku Klux Klan. Davis denied the accusations but Childers, a pro-gun Democrat just like

Scott Murphy, stunningly won the race with 54% of the vote. It was a real test of Obama's popularity and political strength that only became stronger after he was elected president. Tedisco was about to step into the aftermath.

The other logical culprit to Tedisco's problem was President George W. Bush. His administration was like a funnel where the entire GOP was swirling down with him. Tedisco was next.

Get out the Vote

The Tedisco campaign had rented office space in a strip mall in Saratoga County, NY. It was a very large open room with grayish carpeting and bare beige walls. Most campaign workers were too busy to even notice the bland and uninteresting quality of the office. There wasn't much furniture to speak either. A few tables and chairs were strewn about for volunteers to sit on and make phone calls. A few independent rooms were wedged in the rear where those who felt important could have private meetings. The small kitchen was full to the brim with junk food. Trash was piled up sky high near the garbage containers -- a sure sign that people were not as motivated as they were when the campaign first got off the ground. It seemed that there was no fighting left. You could see it in their eyes, in the way they walked, and in their tone regarding the election. "It is what it is," had become a very common phrase.

For some, it felt like a repeat of two years before, almost like déjà vu. Wealthy GE heir Sandy Treadwell had used the same campaign office to run against Kirsten Gillibrand for the very same congressional district. Some of Treadwell's staff volunteered to work for Tedisco. They were back in that campaign office once again feeling the slow crescendo of another failed GOP campaign.

The space next door to the campaign office was in the middle of a renovation. With no carpeting on the floor, the exposed cement was dusty and cold. The walls were not even painted yet. You could see the taped lines where drywalls joined together. That cold and dark spot, was where the Tedisco campaign assembled, what looked like an army of recruits to hit the pavement in a last ditch effort to win the race.

People from all over New York State came out to support the GOP candidate. They were helping themselves to a heaping of free bagels, doughnuts and pastries when Tedisco walked in for his pep talk. "Every poll out there shows this is an extremely tight race which means that I'm going to need your help to cross the finish line," Tedisco said to the volunteers. At this point, the only way to win was to work the streets harder than the other candidate. Whichever side did the best job at getting their voters to the polls would most likely come out on top.

Meanwhile, Murphy was assembling his own army of volunteers. The businessman had come so far from obscurity, he was not about to turn back now. He had President Barack Obama pulling for him. He had New

York Senators Charles Schumer and Kirsten Gillibrand on his corner. He had Bill and Hillary Clinton, the nation's most popular former presidential family at the time, cheering for him. Momentum was building for Murphy.

Newly appointed Democratic Senator Gillibrand, who had achieved rock star status in the 20th Congressional District, came out to support for Murphy. She was a rock star because her approval rating in the district was in the 70's – a clear indication that the people loved her. Democrats were motivated and somewhat confident in their candidate who had narrowed down an insurmountable lead in a heavily Republican district. They were willing to help in anyway possible. But Murphy's campaign still felt the need to beef up its get-out-the-vote efforts with paid volunteers. They were not taking any chances. Labor unions added to the energy with their own manpower on the streets.

Of course, Democrats could afford to lose this one after sweeping the nation just months earlier in the November elections. But no one likes to lose. The election was in the national spotlight. One more Democratic Congressman in the House already in control by a huge Democratic majority would add insult to injury for the GOP. Democrats were enjoying that possibility. Republicans, on the other hand, needed to win this one. With a couple of days left until voters went to the polls, the two campaigns scoured the streets of the 20th Congressional District to get the vote out.

Knocking on doors in a district with close to 700,000 residents was not an easy task. The sheer size of the district made for a difficult recruitment process. Obviously it was impossible to hit every single door. The main goal was to get to as many voters as possible. Republicans were targeting Republicans, conservatives and independents. Democrats went after Democrats, Working Families Party voters and independents.

The GOP was well organized in the 20th Congressional District. The majority of town officials in the district were Republicans. The GOP had tight control over local government jobs. Some residents said that they had to register with the GOP even though they were not Republicans, just to get a town or county job. Helping out the Tedisco campaign meant job security for some. Voter intensity was also a positive sign for the GOP. Republicans wanted to win badly.

Tedisco's team of volunteers were weak in the Northern and Southern portion of the district. In the North Country where Murphy's wife grew up, the campaign office was often empty. The scrum of reporters sometimes outnumbered supporters who showed up for rallies. The North Country also considered Murphy a native son because of his wife's extended family and close connection to the area. His wife was also associated with the Republican Party, which brought support for Murphy from both sides of the isle. In the Southern portion, the Democratic Party was on the rise and well organized. Democrats had already wiggled their way into town and county politics.

According to political scholars, the uptrend for Democrats was the result of a migration of New York City liberals into the district. Tedisco only had the center part of the district locked down. That was where he had the best name recognition. That was where he wanted to make a significant impact in the last minute.

Tedisco was among the hundreds of volunteers pounding the pavement with cautious optimism. His true feelings would often come out in the campaign car, "I don't think we have the numbers. I think we needed a little bit more time to turn this around," he would say in between stops. Poll numbers did suggest that Tedisco had put the breaks on Murphy's momentum. While the independent poll had Murphy leading by four percentage points, other private polls showed Tedisco down by one or two points.

But a Republican strategist from the New York State Senate, a close friend to many in Tedisco's campaign staff said, "I bet, even with a great get-out-the-vote effort, Tedisco loses. He was not the right candidate for that office. It's just too big a campaign for him to get his arms around and he needed to surround himself with better people." That was a common sentiment among many other Republican strategists in New York. They felt that Tedisco's staff was full of rookies who had no business running a congressional race. They were not proven national political campaign winners. In fact none of them had ever been in control of a national race.

District residents were not particularly fond of having campaign workers knock on their doors. They had had enough of Murphy and Tedisco on television ads everyday. They had had enough of the stimulus package, the AIG, American International Group scandal and government bailouts. March was normally a quiet month politically. The nation had always been preoccupied with March Madness. This special election was somewhat of a distraction from the enjoyment of college basketball. Tedisco and Murphy would pop up in the middle of a game during a commercial break to talk about the bad economy, then, ring your doorbell unannounced to ask for your vote. The election was far more important than college basketball. But politicians have attracted so much negative attention over the years that people have become very uninterested.

Those who came to the door thought that Tedisco would win eventually. Some promised to vote for him. Others expressed their disappointments over the negative campaign ads. They also talked about change and the need for new blood in government. It seemed that President Obama's message of change was still resonating even with some Republicans. "I think he's been in office too long," one woman said of Tedisco. "He should give somebody else a chance," she added.

The election was about 12 hours away. Tedisco had decided to pull an all-nighter to make sure he shook as many hands as possible. "When you reach out and touch someone, they are more likely to pull the lever for you than if they had never met you at all," Tedisco said. He was tired and had barely eaten anything. He was functioning on sheer determination. He would go back and forth on the possible outcome of the election. On the one hand he would say, oh yes, I can definitely pull this off if I work hard enough. Then seconds later there was doom and gloom in his eyes. Tedisco spent the overnight hours in Murphy's home base where he visited a manufacturing plant, some diners and WalMart. Late-night employees were surprised to see him. He shook their hands and asked for their vote. "If you want a job, you have to ask for it," he said, referring to the congressional seat.

Murphy's home base was perhaps the area where Tedisco had the weakest. Murphy's home base was perhaps the area where Tedisco had the weakest support. Pulling an all-nighter there was not a bad idea. The race was so close, anything could have tipped the scales. No vote could be spared. One more handshake, one more hug, and one more baby to kiss could translate into more votes and change the outcome of the election. So, from dusk until dawn, the veteran politician was out there meeting and greeting potential voters.

An exhausted Tedisco emerged in the morning once again to fight for his political career. This time the polls were open. Residents were starting to cast their votes. Most people were breathing a sigh of relief that the race was finally ending. The negative and annoying political commercials were finally leaving television screens. The get-out-the

–vote operation was still in full swing. Campaign workers were making a final plea for Tedisco. They focused their attention mostly in Saratoga County and the central portion of the district where Tedisco was expected to score big gains.

The Voters Have Spoken - It's a Tie

L andslide Tedisco was headed home on election night with his Congressional dreams nearly shattered. Tedisco had created that name for himself as a joke after all the votes were counted and was about 60 votes behind Scott Murphy. He was usually pretty funny off-the-cuff. The campaign trail was a riot. The jokes would fly out one after another. He was always quick with comebacks if you pinned a joke on him. That doesn't mean he was ready for the comedy circuit. But he had a decent sense of humor. Most people didn't think landslide Tedisco was funny though. Maybe they didn't get it. One local television reporter thought that Tedisco was going crazy. Here he was trailing Murphy in vote count, and he was talking about a landslide. His supporters laughed nervously. Then, they whispered to each other, "What the heck was that about?

You know... the landslide comment. I didn't get it. Did you?" They were sad to see their candidate looking and sounding almost defeated. "I can't believe it. I can't believe he didn't pull it off," one woman said. "Wow, the Republican Party must really be in bad shape if they couldn't win this seat," another supporter exclaimed. It would take a few days to get over the shock that an experienced campaigner and savvy politician lost to a rookie.

The poll numbers had it right. They predicted a win for Murphy. Tedisco's get-out-the-vote operation might have saved him from an embarrassing night. Political insiders said it might have been one of the best get-out-the-vote efforts they've seen in a long time. Tedisco was down by four percentage points in the polls and he was able to come back for a strong finish. He was out meeting voters overnight and in the middle of the night. He visited every county in the district and met with countless voters. His team of volunteers hit the ground running, stopping at every door possible to trumpet Tedisco's success in the New York State Assembly. But all that effort just wasn't good enough.

Murphy and his supporters were celebrating. There was no victory speech, but you might as well call it a win. His numbers looked good. Any candidate will tell you they'd rather be up than down. The loser always tries to find an excuse. Murphy didn't need any excuses. He would have had a good one too if he needed it. This was a Republican seat anyway, the Democrats would have said. Plus, Murphy was a newbie and Tedisco has been around politics for years. The Democrat businessman had done better than everyone expected. You could see the smiles on their faces and rightly so. Murphy came out of nowhere. He embraced President Obama. By Election Day, his name recognition was as high as Tedisco's. Voters even gave him a higher positive rating than Tedisco according to the last independent poll. The Democrats had every right to celebrate and enjoy the joyous moment. They ran a clever campaign with a good candidate. It was time to reap the fruits of their labor.

What was supposed to be Tedisco's victory party in his hotel banquet room was finally breaking up. The food was gone. The DJ disappeared. The chatter was getting quieter with every ticking of the clock. Hotel workers seemed like they couldn't wait for people to leave.

Tedisco lingered to shake hands after a heartbreaking speech to his supporters. There was nothing but praises for a hard fought battle. "Thank you for your support," Tedisco said with a handshake. People were lined up for a quick greeting – many of them volunteers who had put a lot of their own time into the campaign. They waited their turn patiently one by one slipping in their own words of encouragement. "You did a great job," some said. Tedisco maintained a smile and a positive attitude. "It's not over yet. We still have a long way to go," he said to one volunteer who looked distraught.

It had been quite a night. It was a roller coaster of an election that took the candidates up and down with twists and turns. Tedisco was up then he was down. There were high hopes followed by despair. There were moments of

exhilaration and flashes of discontentment. The veteran politician never imagined that he would be in that situation. No one could have predicted this. It was supposed to be an easy win for Tedisco. After 26 years in state government, he had never been on the losing end. He had thought the seat should come back to Republican hands and this seemed like the perfect moment to snatch it from the Democrats.
The son of the foundry worker who needed this moment to make his father proud was visibly disappointed. The star college basketball player who was often part of a winning team, hated to lose. He hadn't lost this election yet either but his chances didn't look good. He didn't do as well as he had expected in the county where his base was located.

Voting machine re-canvassing which is a process where election workers go over the results under the watchful eye of both campaigns might not do the trick. Mistakes do happen. Election workers sometimes get confused with numbers. They might see a zero and think it's an eight or a three and think it's an eight. A candidate could have accidentally received 500 or 800 extra votes. Many of the election workers at the polls are retired people who can be inaccurate when reading the results out loud. There are usually mistakes on both sides. Machine re-canvassing would fix that problem. These types of mistakes are common. They rarely come into play because the victorious candidate usually wins by a wide margin. In those situations, machine re-canvassing would never change the outcome and would, therefore, be unnecessary.

Tedisco's most trusted advisor, Bill Sherman, tried to make him feel better with encouraging words. "Don't worry, you can make up 60 votes. That's nothing." he said to Tedisco. But he must have had a feeling that Tedisco wasn't going to make it. He must have known that the ship was going down. He had made some arrangements to ensure he didn't go down with the ship. He was angling for another job throughout the campaign and even on the night of the election. His words of wisdom, which are usually worth their weight in gold, didn't work this time. Tedisco's mood remained the same. Other aides piped in with their own consolations "I don't think you have anything to worry about boss. We're going to take this race in the absentees," one said to a sad Tedisco. "We have more absentees than they do. The absentees follow the general election. The military absentees will put us over the top," another aide said.

The fact is, Tedisco's staff and supporters were all worried. Absentee ballots almost always mimic the machine ballots. Statistically, Tedisco was in trouble. But of course, they couldn't tell him that. A victory party was neither the time nor the place to be realistic with a candidate. Keep things positive as long as possible. His team kept a lot from him throughout the campaign, especially bad information. But Tedisco was not an idiot. He knew something wasn't right. Trailing behind was not a good place to be no matter how positive your outlook.

Nonetheless, this was a historic night. This was a key race for the Republican Party – the race that would carve out their path to a comeback. It was the only special contest in the United States, so nearly everyone was paying attention. MSNBC, FOX News Channel, and CNN were all over the story and the possibility of a real tie. Conservative and liberal Internet bloggers were all abuzz about Tedisco's possible demise. Then, it was too close to call – real close. Out of more than 150,000 ballots cast, Scott Murphy was only leading by about 60 votes – making the 20th Congressional District race one of the closest in American history. According to statistics from the Office of the Clerk at the U.S. House of Representatives, there have been more than 20,000 congressional contests nationwide since the organization started to keep track in the 1920's. Less than 50 were decided by fewer than 100 votes.

New York was about to get a taste of what Minnesotans had been going through. The Senate race between Democrat Al Franken and Republican Norm Coleman in Minnesota had come down to a few hundred votes, sparking a long and arduous recount and court battle.[41] The race was one of the longest in American history. The election was held in November 2008. Coleman, the incumbent was ahead by a small margin on election night. After some court decisions and a series of recounts with the lead going back and forth, Franken, a former Saturday Night Live comedian, came out on top. Coleman conceded in June 2009, nearly eight months after the election.

There was a lot riding on this Senate seat. A win for the Democrats meant that they would have a 60-vote filibuster-proof majority in the Senate. Filibuster was the last bit of power onto which Republicans in Washington were holding. The tactic allows them to delay legislative action on any controversial issue by making long speeches. With Franken seated as senator, Republicans had zero power other than the news media.

Political experts were drawing parallels between the Minnesota race and the 20th Congressional District election. Like Minnesota, this race was also important to Republicans. It would mark the beginning of a comeback. Numerous lawyers were already on the phone with Tedisco's campaign on the night of the election. Partisans and election experts were on their way to the district faster than the speed of sound. Tedisco wasn't even out of the banquet room, and his lawyers had already filed paperwork to impound the voting machines. They were trying to avoid a repeat of what had happened in Minnesota between Coleman and Franken. In that race, votes were mysteriously appearing according to published reports. There were suspicions of fraud. The Democrats were blaming the Republicans and vice versa. Tedisco's court order also barred the votes from being recounted without representation from both sides.

PART II - POST-ELECTION

Back to the Phones for More Money

Tedisco woke up the next morning somewhat beside himself. The shock of election night had not worn off yet and he was exhausted from one of the most stressful days of his life. The man who skipped his honeymoon to make sure he didn't miss a day of work at the New York State Assembly really could have used a vacation. He was mentally drained just thinking about the few votes that separated him and his opponent, Scott Murphy. "Can you believe it? 65 votes," Tedisco said, recounting the first election that he ever finished with a virtual tie as a politician.

He was undefeated for more than two decades as a State Assemblyman. He couldn't stop thinking and muttering to himself all the things that he could have done better during the course of the election to change the outcome. He couldn't stop talking about what he could have done differently to convince a couple of hundred more residents to vote for him. It seemed that his mind was racing in different directions. "We didn't have the numbers," he said. He seemed to have been in a world of his own -- preoccupied with regrets.

There was no time for nostalgia. The race was far from over. Tedisco needed more money to keep things going. The campaign office was costly to run and now there were lawyers to pay. The traditional election phase was over. The two campaigns were assembling their army of attorneys to wage war in court. Tedisco had to go back to the phones to ask donors for more money. "I need your help to make sure every vote counts," Tedisco told potential donors. The rhetoric was much the same as in the beginning of the congressional race. "We need a different voice in Washington. We need to stop all the spending the liberal agenda of Rep. Nancy Pelosi."

It was a tough sell. Tedisco had to act confident enough to make donors believe that he would eventually win. He called those who could afford to donate big money on the phone while making a plea to small donors on the Internet with his 20 for 20-campaign. (see chapter 7). He didn't have a problem raising money. Again, a good chunk of the people in the district thought that Tedisco would win the absentee ballots too. More Republicans mailed in their absentees than Democrats according to numbers on the New York State Board of Elections.[42]

Out of 10,000 ballots sent out, more than 6,000 were returned. Tedisco's team had gone out of its way to organize an absentee ballot program. They were aggressive in getting residents to sign up. It might have paid off.

But experts like University at Albany Professor Dr. Alan Chartock said that Democrats have changed their strategy over the years as well with absentee ballots. Republicans used to have an advantage with absentees. Dr. Chartock said that Democrats now specifically target absentee voting as a safety procedure. Perfect timing! That strategy would come in handy in this race. As the saying goes, that was inside baseball. Donors didn't know all the ins and outs. Tedisco raised the money he needed to put up a good fight in court.

While Tedisco and his team of lawyers were waiting for all the absentee ballots to come in, he had some unfinished business to tend to at his day job. His fellow Republican members at the New York State Assembly wanted Tedisco to step down as their leader. They had pent up anger after watching Tedisco pursue the congressional seat full-time while keeping his leadership position. They felt that he was too busy trying to become a Congressman to look out for the minority in the State Assembly.

This fight had been brewing ever since Tedisco announced he was running for Congress. Some members wanted him out then as they were lining up to take his place. According to many political insiders, some of the anger was also generated from the man who would most likely become Tedisco's successor along with Tedisco's own chief of staff, Bill Sherman. The chatter was playing out in the media amid the deadlocked congressional race.

Local newspapers reported the grumbling among State Assembly Republicans, saying that a revolt was imminent. Tedisco wasn't about to quit. He wasn't confident about the outcome of the 20th Congressional District race. Sherman, Tedisco's top advisor who was seen seemingly courting the next leader of the Assembly Republicans, locked Tedisco in a room for a private meeting and managed to convince his boss that stepping down was the absolute right thing to do.

Tedisco's most trusted advisor, the aide that helped him become a Minority Leader, the man who was responsible for his almost every move in the State Assembly and the Congressional race, had turned on him. That's how nasty it had become. He hadn't even lost the race yet, but those who worked for him felt he didn't have the numbers in the absentee ballots. They all scattered away like cockroaches. There was confusion inside the Tedisco circle about who to trust. Everyone around Tedisco was looking over their shoulders, watching out for backstabbers.

Tedisco told reports that he was stepping down as Minority Leader to focus on the recount of the Congressional election. Yes, the recount was extremely important and time consuming but Tedisco remained leader in the Assembly through the lengthy New York State budget negotiations while he was running a national race. It seemed he could have used his multi-tasking skills for the recount as well. On top of that, the New York State budget was done. There wasn't much to deal with anymore at the State

Capitol. It would be a lot easier to go through the recount while maintaining his position as leader of Assembly Republicans. With the state budget out of the way, most lawmakers usually spend less time at the Capitol. There was no real reason to step down other than a big power struggle between those who wanted to be leader.

After washing his hands of the leadership position in the State Assembly, Tedisco had the freedom that he desperately wanted from the beginning of the race. He should have had that freedom to focus on the most important race of his life. He was in his campaign office full time. He was free to make calls day and night to raise money to pay his lawyers. There was one noticeable difference. Very few familiar faces remained. Tedisco was dealing strictly with the folks from Washington D.C. All of his top staff was gone. It was yet another disappointment. They had all gone back to their jobs at the New York State Assembly – leaving Tedisco alone to finish what they had started. Sherman now had a new boss. He was the Chief of Staff for the new Minority Leader in the Assembly after making most of the decisions in Tedisco's Congressional race. It was the first signal that Tedisco was about to fade into obscurity.

Down for the Count

When a race is that close, absentee ballots are under intense scrutiny. Every single one is poked and prodded. Lawyers on both sides find any excuse to set them aside or throw them out completely. A check mark in the wrong spot, an illegible name, or a coffee stain can individually be used as reasons to challenge the validity of a ballot. The idea is to get as many absentees to count for your side and disqualify as many of your opponent's ballots as possible. The task is tedious, even for the lawyers who are making significant amounts of money from this kind of transaction. Teams of lawyers, volunteers, and interns from both camps sat around a table with a chance to look at each ballot to decide how to proceed.

All of this was done very methodically. Only the absentees that are added to the final vote counted are open. Lawyers have to make a decision to challenge a ballot with limited information: name, political affiliation and address. Operatives from both Murphy's and Tedisco's camps did what they could to find out ahead of time how absentee voters cast their ballots. One Republican absentee voter said that he received a phone call from someone trying to figure out how he voted. The two sides wanted to make sure they were knocking out the opponent's ballots instead of their own. The Tedisco campaign had finally begun to figure out that even with more Republican absentees than Democratic ones, the race was swinging Murphy's way. It seemed many Republicans had voted for him.

At Tedisco's campaign headquarters, aides set up a dry erase board to keep track of the absentee vote tally in each county. The numbers were coming in sporadically. Tedisco would be up by a dozen votes, then minutes later a new tally would have him trailing Murphy by dozens of votes. The lead went back and forth almost identical to election night. "The absentees usually follow the voting machines anyway," Tedisco's lawyer, James Walsh, said. "You're probably not going to see much of a difference," he added. That much was true until Columbia County, the area where Murphy had a big advantage on election night, started counting its absentees. Columbia County is in the Southern part of the district where Tedisco had limited support and name recognition. It's also the same area that political insiders believe is changing demographically, where the conservative majority is dwindling. Murphy was expected to post big gains in the absentees there.

Murphy was already leading Tedisco by less than a hundred votes just like on election night. Saratoga County, a stronghold for Tedisco, didn't come up with enough absentee votes for the Republican. The county gave Tedisco less than 200 votes in the final tally. Tedisco's campaign was also counting on military absentees to put him over the top. Out of a thousand military ballots mailed out, only 200 were returned. Tedisco's lawyers even tried to mount a court case to allow more time for the military absentee ballots. It was disappointment after disappointment with Columbia County numbers still to come.

Tedisco was no longer holding out hope, but his lawyers wanted to keep fighting. That's understandable because the longer they fought the more money they made. More than 1200 absentees were objected to and set aside for a court hearing during the course of the counting. The Tedisco campaign had done most of the objections. They knew the majority of those votes would most likely go to Murphy. When New York State Supreme Court Justice James Brands ruled that most of the challenged ballots should be counted, it was checkmate.[43] Tedisco and his team of attorneys knew it. They also knew Tedisco didn't have the numbers when Saratoga County came back weak on the absentees. There was nothing else to do but wait and watch Murphy surge. The dreadful reality of the situation became clearer after a huge chunk of Columbia County ballots went Murphy's way.

A distraught Tedisco had no choice but to give up. The concept had crossed his mind a few times. "We're not going to make it. We don't have the numbers," Tedisco said more than once during the recount. "We fought a good fight but we didn't have the numbers," Tedisco added with his voice now breaking up. The Republican candidate conceded the race to Democrat Scott Murphy nearly a month after the special election took place on March 31st, 2009. Tedisco, who always loved the television news cameras, did not call for a press conference. He called Murphy to congratulate him on his victory. He then released a statement and disappeared for a few days. He included his wife, Mary, in his remarks.

"Ultimately, it became clear that the numbers were not going our way and that the time had come to step aside and ensure that the next congressman be seated as quickly as possible. In the interest of the citizens of the 20th Congressional District and our nation, I wish Scott the very best as he works with our new President and Congress to address the tremendous challenges facing our country. Finally, I would like to express my appreciation to all the volunteers, staff, supporters and – most importantly – my family, for their unending support and prayers. They all poured their blood, sweat and tears into this campaign and for that I am eternally grateful."

The election was fought on the national stage over national issues that included the economy, the stimulus package and the bank bailouts. It was seen as a referendum on President Obama's policies. Many residents of the 20th Congressional District thought it shouldn't have been a contest. "Republicans really needed to win that seat," said one New York State Senator. He was right. The trend didn't look promising for the New York GOP delegation.

New York was down to three Republican representatives out of 29. House Speaker Nancy Pelosi even joked, "Aren't there any Republicans from New York?" Democrats had occupied all statewide political offices. Both houses in the state legislature were under Democratic rule. The GOP was hurting across the country. The 20th Congressional District was supposed to be the turning point but Murphy won the race even after his opposition to executing the terrorists from 9/11 was made public and exploited by the Tedisco campaign. Responses to the loss for Tedisco and congratulatory statements for Murphy came from every where in Washington.

Statement From: Michael Steele, Chairman of the Republican National Committee:

"Jim Tedisco ran a tough, but an ultimately unsuccessful, race in a district that has been carried by a long line of Democrat candidates including President Obama, former Rep. Kirsten Gillibrand, Sen. Clinton, Sen. Schumer, and former Gov. Spitzer. The Republican Party must be competitive in districts like NY-20 if we are going to regain our congressional majorities. While we were unsuccessful in this race, the combined efforts of our candidate, the national and state parties, and NRCC show that the GOP is going to invest the resources necessary to regain the resources necessary to regain our majority in the U.S. House of Representatives."

Statement from: Pete Sessions, Chairman of the National Republican Congressional Committee:

"After a long, hard-fought race, the final result of the New York special election reinforces what our party has known since November -- we have our work cut out for us when it comes to winning in Democrat-held districts. In defeat, there will always be disappointment, but we should not ignore some of the encouraging signs that came out of this race."

Statement from Speaker Nancy Pelosi:

"As Speaker of the House, I congratulate Congressman-elect Scott Murphy on his impressive victory in the race for New York's 20th Congressional District. Scott's victory is a clear indication that Democrats, Independents, and Republicans across the country want to continue moving America in a new direction and reject the 'just say no' policies of Washington, D.C. Republicans. As a high-tech entrepreneur and business leader, Congressman-elect Murphy will bring a wealth of experience to the House, which will be critical as we work to create jobs and strengthen our economy, make health care more affordable and accessible, and do so with the highest standards of accountability and transparency to the taxpayers, just as Scott emphasized in his campaign, and as we in the new direction Congress insist upon.

"Scott Murphy fought through a tough race and showed the kind of tenacity and commitment to public service that will serve him and his constituents well in the Congress. I congratulate DCCC Chairman Chris Van Hollen for his outstanding leadership in helping to elect Scott Murphy. I also want to thank President Obama, Vice President Biden, Governor Paterson, and the entire New York congressional delegation for their strong support of Scott Murphy. I look forward to personally congratulating Congressman-elect Murphy and welcoming him, his wife, Jen, and their three children to the New Direction Congress."

Statement from: Chris Van Hollen, Chair of the Democratic Congressional Campaign Committee:

"Congratulations to Congressman-elect, Scott Murphy, on his remarkable, come-from-behind victory. In this election, voters responded to Scott Murphy's record as a successful businessman who helped to create more than 1,000 jobs and his strong support for President Obama's economic recovery package. In trying to win the NY-20 special election, the RNC, NRCC, and their Republican allies went all in on the losing gamble that voters would prefer their 'just say no' approach to President Obama's bold plans to get the economy back on track. Scott Murphy's victory in this district where Republicans outnumber Democrats by more than 70,000 represents a rejection of the obstructionist agenda and scare tactics that have become the hallmark of House Republicans."

"With his commitment to reaching across the aisle to help President Obama enact his agenda for change, Scott Murphy will be a tremendous asset to our Democratic Caucus. I am grateful to President Obama, Vice President Biden, House Democratic Leaders, Governor Paterson, Senators Schumer and Gillibrand, the entire New York congressional delegation, and DNC Chairman Tim Kaine for their work on behalf of and support of Scott Murphy."

What Went Right, and What Went Wrong

It would seem that Tedisco had everything going for him in the 20th Congressional District special election: **Advantage number one:** His popularity was unmatched by his opponent. No one knew Murphy in the district. Tedisco had been around for nearly three decades, grabbing headlines in newspapers and showing up on the six o'clock news. He also represented a good portion of the most populated county in the district as a New York State Assemblyman.

Advantage number two: This was a special election that took place in less than two months. His opponent had very little time to raise his profile. Tedisco was already a known entity and didn't need a lot of money to introduce himself to people.

Advantage number three: The 20th Congressional District had more registered Republicans than Democrats. The GOP had a 70,000 voter registration edge over the Democrats.

Advantage number four: New York State had an extremely weak Democratic Governor. Mr. David Paterson's poll numbers dropped like a rock after snubbing Caroline Kennedy. The daughter of Camelot was interested in the U.S. Senate seat left vacant by Mrs. Hillary Clinton who became Secretary of State in the Obama Administration.

Paterson appointed then Congresswoman Kirsten Gillibrand instead of Kennedy. Paterson was also facing criticism for poorly handling major deficits in the state budget. The majority of New Yorkers wanted to see him gone. The stage was set for also facing criticism for poorly handling major deficits in the state budget. The majority of New Yorkers wanted to see him gone. The stage was set for a Tedisco win. Tedisco and his team thought they would simply cruise to Washington.

Instead of an easy win, the special election turned out to be one for the record books. It left many political experts, like University at Albany Professor, Dr. Alan Chartock, scratching their heads, trying to figure out exactly how a newcomer like Murphy could gain enough notoriety in just a couple of months to defeat an experienced and well known politician. They are pointing to several factors. The most obvious one may be former President George W. Bush. History dictates that it's normal for the electorate to punish a party when its sitting president is unpopular.

Republicans couldn't get elected after President Richard Nixon resigned amid the Watergate scandal in the 1970's. Today's Republicans have to thank Mr. Bush for their downfall. While the Bush administration was managing an unpopular war in Iraq, the economy was going south, and gas prices were sky-rocketing. Even most Republicans agree that President Bush single-handedly brought down the GOP after his eight years in office. The party lost its majority in Congress in 2006 and kept going downhill. Tedisco was one of many casualties.

President Obama's momentum also lasted quite a while longer than Tedisco and his team had anticipated. The first black president was elected in November 2008, just four months before the special election in the 20th Congressional District. President Obama had won states like Virginia, which are usually Republican strongholds. He took nine states that President Bush won against Senator John Kerry in 2004. The political winds were with the Democrats and their charismatic candidate at the top of the ticket.

They swept the country and gained a super majority in the Senate while riding on Mr. Obama's coattails. Unfortunately for Tedisco, the new president's coattails were still quite long when he jumped into the congressional race. Murphy never missed an opportunity to mention President Obama's name. The President officially endorsed him. He and Tedisco fought over the stimulus package that was signed into law by the president. It appears that Tedisco was going against the strong waves of a well-liked president and lost.

The third factor that played a role in Tedisco's demise was the shift in demographics in the 20th Congressional District. Many political experts wonder if the district should be put in the toss-up category. In 2008, Democrat Kirsten Gillibrand won it with a decisive victory over a known Republican. President Obama narrowly won that district in 2008. The district had been in the hands of Conservative Republicans for years. That's why poll after poll showed that most people thought Tedisco would have won.

A lot of New York City residents, usually registered Democrats, have moved Upstate or have second homes in many Upstate counties. Republicans on the ground in the Southern counties in the district said the GOP is no longer a powerhouse."We've lost Columbia County and some of the others in south of Columbia," they said referring to a decline in GOP leadership and voters. (see chapter 6) Columbia County is essentially where Tedisco lost the race. He simply didn't have the numbers in the Southern counties to overcome Murphy's lead.

Finally, the veteran Republican ran a questionable race. Voters complained about his commercials being too negative. A survey revealed that the public saw Tedisco as the aggressor. Murphy's commercials seemed sharper and well produced while Tedisco's ads didn't resonate with the people of the 20th Congressional District. Tedisco also refused to answer whether he'd vote for the stimulus package. Congressional Republicans had voted no on the bill. Tedisco couldn't go against them nor did he want to do so. He was against the stimulus package because it spent too much.

A simple no to initial media inquiries on where he stood might have been sufficient, but his indecision one way or the other on the bill played out for most of the campaign – giving Murphy an edge on the issue. Dodging the stimulus question validated Murphy's assertion as well that Tedisco was just another career politician who didn't want to be accountable to the people. In the end, for many people who paid attention, Tedisco just wasn't himself. He left the entire campaign up to a team he assembled from his office at the New York State Assembly. Many of them had never run a congressional campaign. By the time Tedisco woke up from the nightmare, it was too late.

The Pendulum Swings

Well, President Barack Obama's coattails were not that long after all. Scott Murphy served a short time in Congress before he was picked off. A year and a half after he was sworn into office with great fanfare, Murphy was defeated in a massive Republican wave that swept the nation.

Two years prior, in 2008, Republicans had trouble getting elected anywhere in the country. The party had no power in Washington. Democrats had complete control of Congress and the White House. What a difference two years can make.

The stimulus program, the bank bail outs, the new healthcare law (The Affordable Care Act), initiatives to save the housing industry and other measures meant to produce jobs -- all created a theme that government was getting too big. The Affordable Care Act became law in March 2010 and was met with mixed reaction. The measure was supposed to increase health insurance coverage for more Americans.

Some people liked it, others didn't and many people just didn't know enough to have an opinion. It was an exhausting two years, marred with battles between Democrats and Republicans in Congress. Meanwhile, people were still losing their homes; and the job market never really improved. The American public was frustrated. They didn't believe claims by economists that the Great Recession was over. So, it appeared they took out their frustrations by lashing out at government. President Obama took the brunt of the criticism. The president's job approval rating was below 50%. It was above 60% right after he was elected, according to the Wall Street Journal.

The special election between Jim Tedisco and Murphy in the 20th Congressional District was in the past. Murphy had become part of the establishment. The fresh-faced businessman approach was pretty much over. He was well known and had been working in Washington on behalf of the people in his district. The Republicans targeted the young congressman before he could even settle into the job. New representatives really don't have a lot of time to get acclimated in Congress. They only serve a two-year term before they have to go back on the campaign trail.

Tedisco often said it's a tough job because members of the House always have to be in campaign mode. "You have to start raising money from the time you get elected for your re-election," he said. "It's even worse for a seat like the 20th Congressional district that's now, more often than not, in the toss-up category." Representatives from those types of districts work for a year. Then they're forced to start raising money to make sure they keep their job. Murphy didn't even get two years. With a special election held in March 2009, he was back on television introducing his family to his constituents all over again.

It seemed the GOP wanted what they believed was rightfully theirs. They had made two failed attempts after Congresswoman turned Senator Kirsten Gillibrand, captured the seat back in 2006 during what was then a Democratic wave. Times had changed and the tables had turned. It happens every midterm election. The party in power almost always takes a hit. Since the Democrats controlled the White House, they were the culprits for America's woes. However, according to many political analysts, the country was not in love with the GOP.[44] Karl Rove, who served as Senior Advisor to former President George W. Bush, said in a Wall Street Journal article "Republicans are on probation." He added that the party needed to deliver on promises it made on the campaign trail in order to get off probation. Polling data suggested people were equally dissatisfied with both parties.

Instead of Tedisco, Chris Gibson was chosen to be the GOP's candidate for the midterm elections. Supporters were convinced Gibson's credentials would give Murphy quite a challenge. Gibson is a retired army Colonel and a combat veteran who spent 24 years in the military. He was deployed seven times, including four tours of duty in Iraq. He's also an author and holds a doctorate degree from Cornell University. He sounded pretty impressive,[45] but Murphy was not too shabby either. He was a millionaire venture capitalist, with a Harvard education.

The race was a lot similar to Tedisco versus Murphy. Instead of the stimulus package, Gibson and Murphy fought over the new healthcare law, another President Obama policy. As a congressman, Murphy had voted against the bill the first time it was brought up in the House. "I voted against the House health insurance reform legislation because it did not adequately address the fundamentally flawed system that has led to skyrocketing health care costs, bankrupt families, and excessive profits for insurance companies," Murphy wrote on his congressional website.

Then, he later voted in support of a different version of the bill. "I voted to pass the President's health insurance reform legislation, which is fundamentally different from the House bill: it will stop the out of control growth of health care costs, protect our local industries and jobs from unfair taxes, and help small businesses create jobs - while cracking down on waste, fraud and abuse."[46]

Republicans and the Tea Party moment had sharpened their claws to attack Democrats in congressional districts nationwide on their vote for the healthcare law. Had Murphy kept his no-vote the second time, would he have been vulnerable? No one will ever know the answer.

Though it seemed that was the trend for many Democrats. The ones who voted for healthcare had a lot trouble getting re-elected. Representatives in Florida, Pennsylvania, New Hampshire, Indiana and Virginia all lost. They all voted for the healthcare bill.[47]

Murphy, as the incumbent in New York's 20th Congressional District, had a sizeable lead in the beginning of the race; almost similar to Tedisco's big edge over him in the special election. No one knew who Gibson was. He had to build up his name recognition and a reputation at the same time.

Murphy and Gibson fought hard with commercials on television. They attacked each other on jobs, taxes, education and Social Security. The two candidates were pretty nasty at times and once again, there were several third party commercials from Democrat-leaning and Republican-leaning organizations trying to make a case for their chosen candidate. It was a no holds barred political exchange.

The biggest difference between Murphy versus Tedisco and Murphy versus Gibson, was timing. Murphy and Tedisco faced-off in a special election. It was the only contest at the time around the country. It was nearly impossible not to pay attention. The television commercials were somewhat annoying to many people. In contrast, Murphy and Gibson were part of a general election story line that said Republicans were poised to win back some power in

Washington. They had tried to stage their first comeback with Tedisco. It didn't work out.

Plus, there were other, more important statewide races in New York State. The governor's mansion was looking for a new occupant. Andrew Cuomo, a former HUD Secretary under President Clinton, the son of former Governor Mario Cuomo and New York's attorney general, ran against a wealthy businessman for governor. Cuomo was declared the winner moments after the polls had closed. The Democrat went into Election Night with a colossal lead in the polls over Republican Carl Paladino.

Every statewide political office was also up for grabs. Senators Chuck Schumer and Kirsten Gillibrand were trying to defend their jobs as well. The season was dominated by Tea Party activism. Anger over the economy and what the Obama administration was doing to solve the problem had given birth to the Tea Party movement. Many Republicans, including Paladino, were backed by the Tea Party. So, Gibson and Murphy had to share the television spotlight with many other political figures. However, Tedisco and Murphy had control over the entire political landscape.

At first, re-election seemed within Murphy's reach. He is a likeable guy. No one really complained about him, except after his first vote against the healthcare bill. Some voters staged a protest questioning Murphy on that vote. Otherwise, political observers say they didn't see any other glaring issues that weakened his candidacy.

But the political winds were clearly against him. After two years of President Obama, voters were apparently looking for another change. The eight years of President George W. Bush had long been forgotten. It was Mr. Obama's economy.

And so it was... With Murphy's loss and countless other Democratic representatives across the country, Republicans stormed the House. They pick up enough seats to move into a solid majority. Minority Leader John Boehner, who campaigned for Tedisco had finally gotten what he'd been looking for all along. He wanted to fire House Speaker Nancy Pelosi and move into her job. The Senate, however, didn't flip. It remained in Democratic hands. Nonetheless, Republicans now had a piece of the action in Washington.

The next day, President Obama admitted in a press conference that he took a "shellacking" on Election Day. The president had a different tone than when he was first elected with a mandate to bring change to Washington. He seemed more humble. It was a big difference from the days when his star power and political clout easily helped Democrats win elections. If Tedisco ran in that climate, regardless of all the mistakes he had made, he's convinced he would have been the Republican Party's comeback kid. And maybe he would have.

Resources

1. Josh Kraushaar, (February 6, 2009) "Republican holds early lead for Gillibrand seat," Politico (Arlington, VA: Allbritton Communications)

2. Siena Research Institute, (March 27, 2009) "Siena New York 20th Congressional District Poll: Murphy Takes 4-Point Lead Over Tedisco in Final Week."

3. Heidi Przybyla, (March 26, 2010) "Obama Spending Plan Faces First Test in New York Race," *Bloomberg*

4. Matt Kelley, (February 25, 2009) "Tax Snafus Add Up For Obama Team," *USA Today*

5. Nick Reisman, (April 2, 2009) "Wait is on for Murphy, Tedisco," *Post Star*

6. Andrew Bernstein, (March 31, 2009) "Today's Election Could Inspire High Turnout," *The Saratogian*

7. Heidi Przybyla, (March 26, 2010) "Obama Spending Plan Faces First Test in New York Race," *Bloomberg*

8. (December 29, 2008) "Caroline Kennedy says she's best for the job." *CNN*

9. Raymond Hernandez, (October 11, 2006) "Upstate Race for House Seat Turns Into a Nasty Fight," *New York Times*

10. Elizabeth Lazarowitz, (February 18, 2009)" Caroline Kennedy goes public again, mum on Gov. Paterson," *Daily News*

11. Raymond Hernandez, (March 8, 2003) "Schumer and Clinton Vie to Share Spotlight," *New York Times*

12. Gallup poll, (June 11, 2009) "Republican Party Down on their party."

13. Tim O'Brien, (January 24, 2009) "Greene County GOP goes with Faso," *Times Union*

14.Randal C. Archibold, (September 7, 2000) "Robert Kennedy Jr. Endorses Hillary Clinton," *New York Times*

15. Maury Thompson, (January31, 2009) "Democratic candidate list shrinks," *The Post Star*

16. David Freedlander, (May 22, 2009)"Why Scott Matter, Republicans and Democrats read the tea leaves of the 20th District win," *The Capitol*

17. David Freedlander, (May 22, 2009)"Why Scott Matter, Republicans and Democrats read the tea leaves of the 20th District win," *The Capitol*

18. David Freedlander, (May 22, 2009)"Why Scott Matter, Republicans and Democrats read the tea leaves of the 20th District win," *The Capitol*

19. David M. Halbfinger, (February 23, 2009) "Stimulus Is Early Focus in Race for Gillibrand's Seat," *New York Times*

20. Heidi Przybyla, (March 26, 2010) "Obama Spending Plan Faces First Test in New York Race," *Bloomberg*

21. Heidi Przybyla, (March 26, 2010) "Obama Spending Plan Faces First Test in New York Race," *Bloomberg*

22. Abdon M. Pallasch, (April 12, 2008) "Obama: God, guns are only refuge of bitter Pennsylvanians," *Chicago Sun Times*

23. (February 26, 2009) "Gillibrand shifts on key gun issue," *Politico*

24. Siena Research Institute, (March 27, 2009) "Siena New York 20th Congressional District Poll: Murphy Takes 4-Point Lead Over Tedisco in Final Week."

25. (November 5, 2008) "Money Wins Presidency and 9 of 10 Congressional Races in Priciest U.S. Election Ever," *OpenSecrets.org*

26. (November 5, 2008) "Money Wins Presidency and 9 of 10 Congressional Races in Priciest U.S. Election Ever," *OpenSecrets.org*

27. David Freedlander, (May 22, 2009)"Why Scott Matter, Republicans and Democrats read the tea leaves of the 20th District win," *The Capitol*

28. Siena Research Institute, (February 26, 2009) "Siena New York 20th Congressional District Poll: James Tedisco Has Early 46%-34% Lead Over Scott Murphy."

29. David Freedlander, (May 22, 2009)"Why Scott Matter, Republicans and Democrats read the tea leaves of the 20th District win," *The Capitol*

30. Steven Greenhouse (January 28, 2009) "Union Membership Up Sharply in 2008, Report Says." *New York Times*

31. James Carville, (2009) "40 More Years: How The Democrats Will Rule The Next Generation," *Simon & Schuster*

32. Associated Press Staff, (January 30, 2009) "Michael Steele Elected RNC Chairman," *USA Today*

33. John Avlon, (June 20, 2008) "How the Party of Lincoln was Left Behind on Civil Rights," *Real Clear Politics*

34. Christopher Orlet, (September 24, 2008) "Dinner Politics THE NATION'S PULSE."

35. Amy S. Clark, (October 31, 2008) "Nasty Campaign Ad Spending Beats Nice 10:1," *CBS News*

36. Leigh Hornbeck, (April 26, 2009) "Lack of unity fatal to Tedisco Republicans split in nominating contest for House; the "no" factor," *Times Union*

37. Siena Research Institute, (March 27, 2009) "Siena New York 20th Congressional District Poll: Murphy Takes 4-Point Lead Over Tedisco in Final Week."

38. Siena Research Institute, (March 12, 2009) "Siena New York 20th Congressional District Poll: Murphy Cuts Tedisco's Lead From 12 to 4 Points."

39. Siena Research Institute, (March 12, 2009) "Siena New York 20th Congressional District Poll: Murphy Cuts Tedisco's Lead From 12 to 4 Points."

40. Siena Research Institute, (March 27, 2009) "Siena New York 20th Congressional District Poll: Murphy Takes 4-Point Lead Over Tedisco in Final Week."

41. Eric Black, (April 1, 2009) "Coleman Franken Redux in New York?" *MinnPost.com*

42. "Unofficial Combined Machine and Paper Results for NY 20th Congressional District," (April 23, 2009) *New York State Board of Elections*

43. Elizabeth Benjamin, (April 6, 2009) "Let the Counting Begin!" *Daily News*

44. David Paul Kuhn (November 3, 2010) "Exit Polls: Unprecedented White Flight from Democrats" *Real Clear Politics*

45. ChrisGibsonForCongress.com

46. scottmurphy.house.gov/Issues/Issue/

47. Julian Pecquet (November 2, 2010) "Few Democrats Survive Healthcare Vote" *The Hill*

OTHER SOURCES

1. Jennifer A. Dlouhy, (29 April 2009) "Murphy sworn in surrounded by his 'very large family,'" *Times Union*

2. Maury Thompson, (January 24, 2009) "Saratoga County GOP backs Tedisco," *The Post Star*

3. David Halbfinger, (April 1, 2009) "No Decision Soon in Upstate House Race," *New York Times*

4. "Total Enrollment by Congressional District," (January 28, 2004) *New York State Board of Elections*

5. Michael Barone, (January 28, 2009) "Political Bloodlines of Kirsten Gillibrand, Senator From New York," *U.S. News & World Report*

6. James L., (January 23, 2009) "NY-20: Traditionally Red District Turned Blue in 2008," *Swing State Project*

7. Joseph Spector, (March 25, 2009) "Obama For Murphy," *Politics on the Hudson*

8. Jonathan Martin, (March 25, 2009) "Biden cuts radio ad in New York race," Politico (Arlington, VA: Allbritton Communications)

9. Casey Seiler, (January 27, 2009) "Paterson: No hard time-line for 20th special election

10. John Bresnahan, (March 11, 2009) "Dem closing in key N.Y. House race," Politico (Arlington, VA: Allbritton Communications)

11. Sam Stein, (March 25, 2009) "Obama Flexes Political Muscle, Enters NY Congressional Race," *Huffington Post*

CPSIA information can be obtained at www.ICGtesting.com
Printed in the USA

268816BV00004B/106/P